The Classic
Kissel Automobile

by Val V. Quandt

First Edition

Library of Congress Catalog Card Number: 90-92249

ISBN: 0-942495-08-X

Kissel Graph Press
147 N. Rural Street
Hartford, WI 53027

Printed in the United States of America by
Palmer Publications, Inc.
Amherst, Wisconsin 54406

To the memory of Louis Kissel

iv

Table of Contents

Acknowledgements

I am indebted for assistance and source materials for this preparation to the memoirs of the late William L. Kissel, one of the original founders of the Kissel Motor Car Company, and his family of Robert, Sr., Robert, Jr., and William W. Kissel, the Herman Palmer family for his records, Beatrice Kissel Schauer and Fred Schauer for their generous support for this project, and the Hartford Heritage Auto Museum, Betsy Kissel Schultz, James W. Kissel, Gene Husting, for his long standing interest in the Kissel Kar Klub and his large contributions of Kissel materials useful for this study, Ralph Dunwoodie, a fellow founder of the same club and continuing contributor of Kissel historical materials, Delyle Beyer and Dave Lanning for their contributions to the Kissel heritage through their expertise in Kissel vehicle restorations, Dale Anderson as director of the Hartford Heritage Auto Museum and the archives of this museum, Mike Schuetz and the Washington County Historical Society, the City of Hartford Public Library History Collection, Chet Krause and John Gunnell of Old Cars Weekly and the Standard Catalog of American Cars, 1805 to 1942, and other numerous donors of Kissel memorabilia to the Hartford Heritage Auto Museum in Hartford, Wisconsin. Carol Orth is to be thanked for her careful word processing work in preparing this material.

Finally, I wish to acknowledge and thank Peter J. Quandt, my son, of Newbridge Communications, Inc., whose suggestions were of prime influence in my getting started on this project, and my wife, Faith, for her patient encouragement of my efforts.

Preface

It has been nearly 60 years since the last Kissel automobile left the plant of the Kissel Motor Car Company in Hartford, Wisconsin. What was a 25-year production of nearly 35,000 passenger cars, trucks, and other commercial vehicles, has now dwindled to a remnant of around 200 Kissel cars. Many of this number are not whole cars, but rather portions of vehicles, such as a chassis.

Some 182 Kissel Kar Klub members own the majority of the above number of vehicles. A few other Kissels exist in the hands of owners who have not registered with the Kissel Kar Klub.

In the past, numerous articles have been written on the subject of the Kissel automobile. Especially has this been the case with the subject of the early classic roadster, the Kissel Speedster. Shown in the color of chrome yellow it was affectionately known as the Gold Bug. Greater amounts of material are now available and have been utilized to allow for a larger, more encompassing work on this famous, and still highly regarded automobile.

It deservedly maintains its designation as a classic in its time, and true to the Webster definition of the term as being "of the highest class, and a model of its kind."

With the background of the writer as a medical practitioner, and now archivist for the Kissel material since the inception of the Hartford Heritage Auto Museum, it has neither been a desire, or indeed possible, to approach the subject of the Kissel with a heavy emphasis only on mechanical details. An attempt was made to keep factual errors to a minimum, knowing however, that this would not always prove to be possible. It is hoped that this presentation will give the reader a true appreciation of the Kissel, where it stood in the automobile ranks in its time, and especially, also in its setting and relationship to some of the outstanding events occurring in the same time period, not the least of which was the First World War.

Val Quandt
Hartford, Wisconsin
December, 1990

Introduction

My exposure to Kissel goes back to 1920, when, as a boy of ten, I was living in Fond du Lac, Wisconsin. This is some forty miles north of Hartford where Kissels were built. At that time I regularly visited an aunt and uncle there and at nearby Pike Lake, sharing vacations before they had their own children. I vividly recall Kissel chassis barrel out on Branch Street's dusty road breaking in or testing Kissels before the bodies were mounted, and then also the later completed vehicles. I was caught up in "Gold Bug Fever" as they passed by in a final test. They were striking, low racy beauties.

My uncle had a prosaic Ford Model T, but his parents gave him access to their 1918 Kissel 100-Point Six All Year Sedan, and I had many rides in it. I remember its throaty sound of power and the smoothness of its ride. The detachable All Year winter enclosure, as described in most literature, stayed on this car the year around. The top was secured so tightly that I recall ear discomfort unless a window was opened an inch or two. They had an elegant look, reflecting much attention to details, and a finish that spared no expense. Although our bread and butter came through the employment of my father with the Buick Division of General Motors Corporation, and my first car was a 1924 Buick Four Roadster, I was a Kissel fan and still am.

My first Kissel was not to be until 25 years later when I bought and restored an incomplete, weathered, but very low mileage 1920 Kissel Speedster. This was one of the famous "Gold Bugs" which, after I located another in near original condition, I sold to a lawyer friend of Kissel's talented head of design and production, William L. Kissel, who was the number two man in the Kissel Motor Car Company from its beginning in 1907. The new owner kept the car at his summer home in Belgium, Wisconsin, a dozen miles from Hartford. There Will drove the car several times, and once I was present with a camera.

My second Kissel, a slightly older 1920 model of the Gold Bug became available to me in Rhode Island in reasonably good condition. It had been driven by its owner and family until 1952, two wheel brakes and all. Eventually the Harrah Collection bought it away from me. How I wish I had one now!

Dr. Quandt is particularly qualified to be the official authority on Kissel's history, where, retired from his medical practice, in touch with some of the Kissel family and old company people, able and dedicated to his subject, he has all the resources for a penetrating examination of the car and the Kissel company. Through the depth of his research he is able to resolve some conflicting material or statements which seem to be the rule everywhere where people's memories are tested after the lapse of a long period of years. He was particularly fortunate in having access to local newspaper articles blanketing the whole life of Kissel from its early years until its inevitable failure along with so many of the other "independents" in the Great Depression of the 1930s. His is a balanced account of what one early Kissel historian or author described as "a great American company, German flavor." Here, in my opinion, is the definitive Kissel history.

Gene Husting
Long Island, New York

x

Chapter One

Origins of the Kissel Motor Car Company

The Kissel automobile, while known to the collector as a classic, is unknown to the vast majority of the American public today. It had its origin and most of its life history at a time when there were literally hundreds, and during an early time, thousands of automobile manufacturers in America. Most of these companies were relatively small as was Kissel, and a large number of them made just one or a handful of vehicles. The Kissel marque today is distinguished by being in the listings of the Classic Car Club of America for some of its models. Most famous was its racy looking roadster, affectionately known as the "Gold Bug."

The Kissel automobile was manufactured in Hartford, Wisconsin, from 1906 and model year 1907 until 1931, although technically the company had folded and went into receivership in September of 1930. Amongst other reasons, it was the victim of the economic depression following 1929 which heightened the problems of the small manufacturer.

Hartford, in 1906, had a population of just 3,000 people, and this figure had just doubled in the preceding decade. The early immigrants were largely of German origin, then Irish. The German wave of immigrants came to America, starting in 1848, following the economic and political upheavals taking place in Germany at this time. Numbered among these was Louis Kissel who came to America in 1857 and settled in the northern portion of Washington County called Addison Township. He moved to Hartford in 1883, where he owned and operated a hardware store and a farm implement business.

In 1890 he took into partnership his four sons, Adolph P., Otto P., William L., and George A. Kissel. In 1892 and 1893 he purchased what was then the Hartford Plow Works from J.R. Rice and E.G. Rowell. In 1905 he and his sons bought out S.M. Seeley and A.D. Rowell of the plow firm, thus totally owning this business. This activity had now expanded to four large buildings which were devoted to manufacturing and distributing farm machinery, and selling gasoline engines furnished by the Western Malleable and Grey Iron Manufacturing Company of Milwaukee. The Kissel brothers and their machinists were also beginning to work at developing their own gasoline engine.

This early photograph showed a stationary gasoline engine sold by the Kissel Manufacturing Company at a time prior to their manufacture of automobiles. They manufactured some farm machinery and they acted as distributors for others. Picture courtesy of C.T. Wendel, in American Gasoline Engines.

Brothers Adolph and Otto were to occupy themselves with home building and sales, and farm sales. At this early time they owned some 500 choice residential lots in Hartford. Between 1906 and 1912 they had built 300 homes. New employees of Kissel were encouraged to purchase these homes. The Kissels had their own stone quarry and sand pit in and near Hartford. They brought down logs

This Louis Kissel family picture was taken in about 1894, with sons and future Kissel Motor Car Company heads, Will and George flanking left and right, respectively.

from northern Wisconsin. In their facilities they had mills for producing their own finishing lumber. They built many of their home components such as window frames. Since all Kissel automobiles, later, had wooden frames, this wood processing was an integral part of their plans.

In 1903 Kissel brothers Otto, Will, and Adolph, all in their early twenties, were interested in buying a 1903 Orient Buckboard. Instead they chose to buy a 1904 White Steamer, a larger car, which they purchased in Milwaukee, Wisconsin. The enthusiastic and energetic brothers then became an informal small agency to sell the White Steamer in the Hartford area. They sold three of these for $2,000 each and at a profit of $400 apiece. This fueled their appetite to launch into the automobile manufacturing business, or at least to build a car.

The very first Kissel car came about with the help of a pattern maker in their Hartford Plow Company. This was Sam Toles, who made up drawings and specifications for a four-cycle gasoline engine of 18 to 20 horsepower. The brothers, George and Will, made the engine castings and built the four-cylinder engine. They were delighted to see that it ran. Then they made up much of a crude roadster body and bought the other necessary components such as the frame, axles, transmission, steering gear, wheels, and radiator. They gave the vehicle a trial run around Hartford and then turned it over to Sam Toles as a gift.

With this meager experience, the Kissel brothers, Will, age 27 years, and George, age 25 years, in the spring of 1906 decided to go into the automobile manufacturing business. Reminiscing later, Will Kissel recalled that they were then familiar with many of the automobiles of the time, such as the Pierce-Arrow, Locomobile, Peerless, Stoddard Dayton, Royal Tourist, Packard, Pope Toledo, White, Stanley Steamer, Winton, Jeffery, Cadillac, Ford, and Franklin, to name a few.

This was the first Kissel assembled automobile made by brothers George and Will Kissel with parts then available and with practical assistance of one of their employees, Sam Toles. It was a four-cylinder.

They produced a sample car of purchased units including a Beaver four-cylinder engine, Warner amidships transmission, Timken axles, Smith frame, cone clutch, and steering gear. They had the body designed and manufactured by L.E. Zimmermann Company of Waupun, Wisconsin, which resembled the two seater Portland cutter. This company had been building these bodies for their horse drawn vehicle trade. This assembled vehicle was successfully driven and it was sold to Mr. E.C. Savage of Milwaukee, their first customer. He quit his job as a traveling salesman and became their Milwaukee agent for future sales.

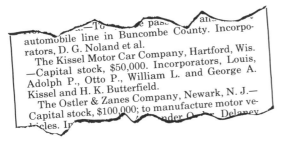

This announcement of the incorporation of the Kissel Motor Car Company appeared on June 20, 1906 in a publication aptly called The Horseless Carriage.

In early 1906 plans were being drawn for the start of a new automobile manufacturing company. The company needed organizing. The first meeting to form the Kissel Motor Car Company took place in Hartford on June 25, 1906. It was incorporated with a capital stock of just $15,000 paid in, as Will Kissel described it in his memoirs, although an additional $35,000 soon flowed in from H.K. Butterfield and others for a total of $50,000, as has generally been quoted. Officers elected were: Mr. H.K. Butterfield, a United States district attorney as president, Otto P. Kissel as vice-president; and George A. Kissel as secretary and treasurer. George Kissel, just 25 years of age, was chosen to manage the company with help from his father, Louis. Brother Will was to assist him. Early plans called for a touring car and a runabout. Instead it made only touring cars for Joseph McDuffee of Chicago. McDuffee was an auto dealer for Stoddard Dayton and Royal Tourist. He heard about the enterprising Kissel activity in Hartford. He came to check out the car and brought

This vehicle, produced in 1906, was the prototype for the 100 vehicles manufactured for the Joseph McDuffee agency of Chicago. The body was furnished by the Zimmermann Company of Waupun, Wisconsin, which had been making bodies for the horse drawn trade.

along Joseph A. Tarkington, who was his superintendent of shops in Chicago. They came in one of their Stoddard Daytons, and asked that the Kissels pattern a vehicle after this model. Tarkington stayed on with the Kissels to supervise manufacture of the Kissel new car. This turned out to be an order for 100 vehicles to be delivered by July of 1907. Kissel came within about a month of meeting this deadline.

At the end of this production there was a chassis left over that was made into a runabout for the personal use of Will Kissel. The McDuffee Automobile Company in their February, 1907 publicity brochure stated clearly what they wished to promote in selling the new KisselKar, as it was called. "In designing the KisselKar the condition of American roads with their frequent steep grades, long stretches of sandy soils, and otherwise heavy traveling was taken into consideration. Also taken into account was the fact that today the owner wishes to drive the car himself or wishes his wife or children to run it without employing a chauffeur. Thus, in order to afford the complete and safe enjoyment of motoring, it necessitates a strong and light-weight car with ample power, and one which is ever-ready, instantly responsive, and always reliable." The first run for the McDuffee order was the "C" KisselKar. It was a touring car. The very first of the McDuffee order was shipped out to Chicago on December 11, 1906.

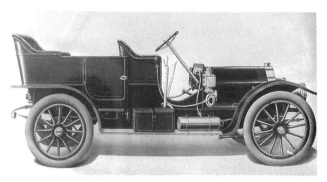

This was the first KisselKar, Model "C", produced for
Jos. McDuffee, and as it appeared in his sales literature.
It had a 96-inch wheelbase and weighed 2,250 pounds.

For those readers mechanically inclined, the following information on specifications will be of interest:

THE 1907 "C" KISSELKAR

Motor:	Four cylinders, vertical, cast in pairs, 30 H.P.
Cylinders:	4½-inch bore, 4¾-inch stroke
Transmission:	Sliding gear type, selective system, three forward speeds, and reverse. Timken roller bearings throughout
Rear Axle:	Floating type, Timken roller bearings throughout
Front Axle:	Constructed of heavy Shelby seamless drawn tubing with extra heavy drop forged knuckles
Frame:	Pressed steel, 98-inch wheelbase
Springs:	Front 42-inch long, rear 46-inch long
Lubrication:	Mechanical oiler, positively driven
Driving shaft:	With large bevel gears, and bevel gear differential
Ignition:	Storage battery, jump spark
Brakes:	Internal and external double acting on the rear wheel hubs
Wheels:	32-inch artillery
Tires:	4-inch, quick detachable
Tread:	56 inches
Seating capacity:	Five persons
Carburetor:	Schebler
Radiator:	Tubular with fan
Weight:	2,250 pounds
Equipment:	Side lamps, set of tools, horn
Price:	$1,850 f.o.b. Hartford, Wisconsin

Kissel called its new car the KisselKar. An earlier conception that the first Kissel was called the Badger was later disproven, having been found to be the creation of a writer of an automotive magazine at the time.

Wisconsin is known as the Badger state. Badger cars are listed and described in the authoritative Standard Catalog of American Cars, 1805-1942, published by Old Cars Weekly in Iola, Wisconsin. Here, indeed, there was an automobile named Badger, produced in the small town of Columbus, Wisconsin in 1910 and 1911. Also, in Clintonville, Wisconsin the Four-Wheel Drive Company in its early history in 1909 called their vehicles the Badger, or the F.W.D. Badger. By 1911, the name was shortened to F.W.D. There was also a Badger Steam Car made in Kenosha, Wisconsin in the year 1901.

In the early days of automobile manufacture it was not unheard of to have several vehicles with the same name or parts of names. Such was the case with another vehicle named Kar, the Kline Kar, made in this country from 1910 to 1924.

The name KisselKar was the official name of the Kissel product until mid summer of 1918. Then anti-German sentiment engendered by the European or First World War caused the factory to drop the Kar of the name. In spite of this the name KisselKar hung on for a period longer such as the description of the Kissel plant as the KisselKar factory. Also there was no consistency in the printed materials. That is, it might appear as **the bisected word form of Kissel Kar, or the**

This was the original motor in the 1907 Model "C" KisselKar,
thirty horsepower, four-cylinder, cylinders cast in pairs,
L-Head.

contracted form of KisselKar. Up until this time the radiator medallion placed on the upper right radiator core stated "KisselKar, Every Inch a Car." After the deletion of the KisselKar name the medallion depicted Mercury, the Greek mythology messenger god.

The Kissels were busy in 1906 making several large additions to their manufacturing space. This was repeated frequently as time went on and the need arose. George Kissel was instrumental in getting auto dealers to be familiar with his KisselKar. In addition to McDuffee in Chicago, other contacts were made for new dealers. George Kissel personally attended the national auto shows to exhibit the Kissel offerings. He attended the auto show held in New York in January of 1907 with two Kissels, one red with red leather upholstery and the other dark green with gold striping. At the time, he left behind a factory work force of 125 men, and a factory that was supplied with 24-hour a day electricity generated in the Kissel factory.

Hill climbing contests were indulged in by the early car manufacturers to help promote their products. Kissel entered numerous contests, often with George Kissel at the wheel. A KisselKar defeated a Stoddard Dayton in two of three hill climbs in Milwaukee in 1907. An early endurance test had George Kissel at the wheel of a KisselKar driving from Milwaukee to Madison and return without mishap.

The chief engineer for chassis, including engines for the early Kissels, was found through unusual circumstances. Mr. Herman Palmer happened to be passing through Hartford, Wisconsin on a train. He noted the big factory site and decided to inquire for a job. He worked as a bench hand, not mentioning his college degree from Germany in engineering studies. He was called into consultation when

This was an early advertisement for the new 1907 KisselKar, which appeared in the publication called Motor Age, on January 24, 1907. McDuffee had his automobile agency in Chicago on Michigan Avenue, with a branch office in Milwaukee. Picture courtesy of Ralph Dunwoodie.

KISSEL KAR

❧ If you are familiar with the points that give **any** automobile real claims to excellence—no matter what its price—we'd just like to go over Kissel Kar with you and show you that it has all of them. And it **sells for one-third to nearly two-thirds LESS.**

Makers:
KISSEL MOTOR CAR CO.
Hartford, Wis.

Address all correspondence to
McDuffee Automobile Co.
SOLE AGENTS

Chicago—Michigan Ave.
at 15th St.
Milwaukee—228-232 Wisconsin
Street

This 1908 touring KisselKar had the driver seated on the left side with his controls, in contradistinction to the usual practice of having the driver on the right side. This continued to be the case into 1913. This touring car shows the hand brake and the primitive bulb horn outside the seating compartment, and the shift stick just inside. Carbide headlamps were the standard. The horsepower had been increased to 40.

he heard that certain drawings needed to be made for their Warner starting motor gear. Palmer supplied the necessary expertise to solve the problem. Thus, he started his long career with the Kissel Motor Car Company as their head mechanical engineer.

Production of the 1908 KisselKar models was begun in July of 1907, at the time that the 1907 McDuffee order was nearing completion. These consisted of a four-cylinder vehicle, offered in body styles of touring, roadster and limousine. Horsepower was increased from 30 to 40. Engine displacement was slightly increased by the square configuration of 4¾-inch bore and 4¾ inch stroke. The wheelbase was increased from 96 inches to 108 inches. In 1908 Kissel changed its radiator outline design from one with a rounded arc on top to one more angular. This was of a hexagonal shape, with most of this shaping on top. Headlamps were powered by Prest-O-Lite canisters of acetylene made by the company of this name in Indianapolis, Indiana.

To promote these cars George Kissel made a trip to New York City where he completed a

contract with E.B. Gallaher for 100 cars. On his return trip he stopped in Chicago and finalized a contract with Jay Webb, the famous race driver, for 150 cars for the central territory, which Joe McDuffee had vacated for Watrous, New Mexico. By 1908 some of the body work was transferred to the Charles Abresch Company in Milwaukee. A 1908 KisselKar was sold to be used by the daughter of

This original factory photo has survived showing the roadster model of the same period.

This elegant KisselKar had a body made by the Charles Abresch Company of Milwaukee, Wisconsin. Except for the early Zimmermann and Abresch bodies, the KisselKar bodies were to be shortly all designed and produced by the Kissel Motor Car Company, and by Fred Werner who had begun employment with them as head body engineer.

Judge S.W. Lamoreux of Beaver Dam, Wisconsin. It may have been a sign of the male dominant perception that the judge stated that his daughter was one of the few ladies in the state who could drive their own car.

Kissel was out proving its laurels in March of 1908 in a hill climbing contest at Pasadena-Altadena, California where it won over expensive cars in the class of White, Thomas Flyer, Apperson, and Packard.

George Kissel came close to death or at least serious injury on January 27, 1908 when the Kissel rail siding track was the scene of an accident. The engineer of the train claimed that steam from the train boilers obscured his vision when he slammed into the siding track

This page appeared in the publication, Cycle and Automobile Trade Journal, *in May of 1908. The Pacific KisselKar agencies were leaders in promoting the Kissel product. Picture courtesy of Ralph Dunwoodie.*

ramming four railroad cars which were parked there to receive new KisselKars. The force of the collision pushed the railway cars over the end of the track through the factory wall and into the interior of a machine stock room that over the noon hour was occupied by a stock clerk and George Kissel, who was working at his desk. The force of the protrusion struck Kissel, but he escaped with minor bruises.

On April 19, 1908, Louis Kissel, who was 69 and the father of George and Will, was shot by an angry employee. He died nine days later in a Milwaukee hospital. Louis Kissel was still active in the hardware division of the family business. He was working in the hardware store in downtown Hartford when he was assailed by a French Canadian by the name of John Gerbier. This man was disgruntled, and it was found later upon examination by physicians that he suffered from paranoia. Briefly, the facts were that he wished to purchase a small home from the Kissels when he came to work for them. He had paid down the sum of $200. He worked as a molder and had smashed 40 molds in anger when things did not suit him. He was then given a job in the Plow Works which paid less. That and the fact that he wanted to retrieve the $200 he had put down on his home put him in an angry rage. He was noted to be carrying a revolver for several days before the shooting. His explanation to his fellow workers was that he **intended to take the gun home to clean it.**

Gerbier came into the hardware store and embroiled Louis Kissel in an argument over his alleged grievances and shot him in a fit of anger. Of three shots fired, one penetrated his abdomen, severing the bowel in multiple places. He was taken by train the same day to Milwaukee where surgery was done to repair the internal lacerations. But with the inevitable bacterial contamination, peritonitis followed in this era before antibiotics were discovered, and death soon followed. Gerbier, after his trial, was placed in an institution for the criminally insane.

George Kissel attended auto shows again in New York, in January of 1909 and Chicago in February of 1909 to show his 1909 KisselKars. This model year increased the number of offerings, and it required further building additions to accommodate this growth. In this year two new models were added to meet the demand of the public. There was a four-cylinder car of thirty horsepower selling at $1,500 and a six-cylinder car selling at $3,000. All told, there were thirteen body styles with the smallest at 107 inch wheelbase in four cylinders and 30 horsepower, and offered in a five-passenger touring, baby tonneau, and a

The 1909 KisselKar buyer had a choice of three models in the four-cylinder size. The D-9 and E-9 came with a 40 horsepower engine, and there was offered the LD-9, which was a smaller four-cylinder with 30 horsepower. Also in this model year, the first six-cylinder car was placed on the market by the Kissel Motor Car Company. Shown here is a factory picture of the D-9, in a touring model.

coupe all called LD-9. There was an intermediate size D-9, and E-9, with 115-inch wheelbase, 40 horsepower, 36-inch wheels, and offered in touring, limousine, roadster, coupe, and baby tonneau. The largest size was the G-9 model six-cylinder with 60 horsepower, wheelbase of 130 inches, and offered in five and seven passenger touring, limousine, roadster, coupe, semi-racer, and a baby tonneau with a top price of $4,200 in the G-9 limousine, and the least expensive at $1,350 in the single seat LD-9.

The KisselKar Model E-9 was in the middle cost range, here shown in the Coupe. It had a four-cylinder engine shared with the D-9 series.

This G-9 six-cylinder KisselKar had the 60 horsepower engine, and shows the carbide headlamps. Kissel used the commercial fuel supply called Presto-Lite. This limousine carried the high price tag of $4,200.

Kissel had its Semi-Racer model, with its distinctive bucket seats, and the gasoline cylinder situated right behind these seats.

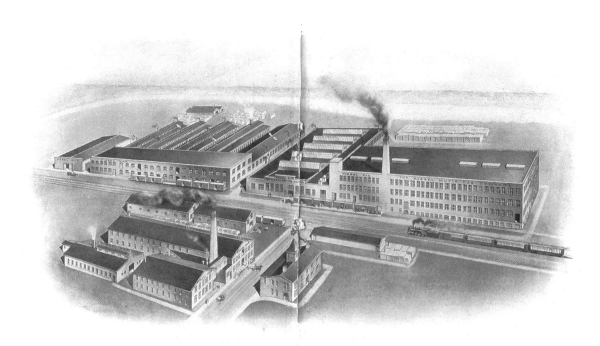

This artist drawing showed the Kissel Motor Car Company as it existed in 1909. Railroad sidings were those of the Chicago, Milwaukee, and St. Paul Railroad. An ambitious start had already been made to becoming a million square foot manufacturing plant. Portions of this structure have survived uses through a succession of outboard motor builders.

This KisselKar Model LD-9 was the small four-cylinder vehicle as shown in this roadster. At a low cost of $1,350 it was a price below which, with minor exceptions, Kissel never ventured.

The most unusual and striking model, also appearing in the models of other manufacturers, was the semi-racer. This had two bucket shaped seats, a slanted oval gas tank right behind these seats, and a tool chest and a cylinder for headlight fuel on the right side running board.

All motors in the 1909 models had valves on one side operated by a single camshaft, with cylinders cast in pairs. These were thus L-head engines.

In its early production years Kissel did not concentrate much production and publicity on its trucks. The very earliest around 1908 and 1909 were basically one of a kind using a passenger car chassis. Kissel described one which was a large wooden box fastened to one of their long wheelbase passenger chassis. Later, by 1910, there were trucks of special design. The development of the KisselKar trucks, as they were called, will be described in the unfolding of the Kissel Motor Car Company development designed to meet the market.

The following is an account that appeared in the January of 1909 issue of the New York American Magazine. It is humorous and shows to what extent a KisselKar dealer went to publicize his car. F.S. Dickinson, the New York manager for the KisselKar, made a wager with a friend of his that he would take a KisselKar up to the top of an 18-story roof top. The inference was that it would be driven up. This was the old Fifth Avenue Hotel at 23rd Street and Fifth Avenue. What then happened was that Dickinson had the vehicle hoisted to the top of the building, with a chauffeur in place. The trip to the building top and return to the ground was made without mishap, to the applause of a street audience, and the dismay of the local police.

The 1909 KisselKar was the first to have a round medallion in the right upper radiator core, mentioned earlier, with the inscription, "KisselKar, Every Inch a Car."

The Kissel Motor Car Company endured a harrowing experience when the family-owned Hartford Plow Works adjacent to the auto manufacturing plant had its three buildings totally destroyed by fire. The fire endangered but caused no damage to the auto plant. The entire insurance replacement loss for the buildings and contents came to just $30,000.

The Kissel logo shown as a radiator medallion lasted from 1909 until late 1918 when the Teutonic sound of Kar met with public disfavor and the ornament was changed to Mercury, the Greek mythology messenger god.

Chapter Two

The KisselKar
Every Inch A Car

14

At this point, it might be useful to reflect on a development parallel to that of the automobile industry and that was closely allied to it and equally necessary. This was the manufacture of tires, tubes, rims, and wheels. The vulcanization of rubber was a process known before the beginning of this century. In this process crude rubber is subjected to heat with sulfur or its compounds to make it nonplastic and increase its strength and elasticity.

Early tires were solid, especially for heavy duty hauling as was evident in this use for the early trucks. The idea of folding the rubber into a tube to make a pneumatic tire had its first practical use in Scotland with John Boyd Dunlop in the manufacture of a bicycle tire.

In this country names such as Firestone, Goodyear, and Goodrich are well known as pioneers in the tire industry. Charles Goodyear did early experimenting in developing a useful tire. This involved the use of many different chemicals, and cloth fibers to make the tire durable and pliable. Goodyear helped pioneer the use of a practical valve in connection with the inner tube of the pneumatic tire.

The early tires tended to slip on their rims. It was a common sight to see tires slipping on their rims as on the incline of a hill.

In an attempt to hold the tire on the rim various solutions were attempted. There was the early Clincher tire with a metal bead to be drawn tightly around and against the rim. Demountable rims were devised that allowed the motorist to have tires mounted on these rims as spares in the event of a tire failure on the road. This was exceedingly common. Early in this century there was an average of a tire failure within 5,000 miles or less. By 1915 the average was close to a tire failing after 8,000 to 10,000 miles. By this time the improvements were in the fibers used in the tire construction with ever increasing sophistication. In time fibers used changed from natural substances such as cotton to tougher synthetic cords.

Charles Courtney, of Hartford, Wisconsin, owned this modified touring car, called the "Rubber Neck," referring to its use as a small sightseeing bus. The radiator displays the new medallion. This picture is from the Will Kissel collection who in 1957 identified all the vehicle occupants and the bystanders.

This 1910 model was a commercial KisselKar used as a delivery van. The early Kissel trucks and vans shared most of their chassis components with their passenger cars.

The need to put a tread on the tire became apparent with the problem of slippage with the early tires. Harvey Firestone, who lived 1868 to 1938, had the first tread tire in America. He had the elevated imprinting "Non Skid" placed over the whole tire circumference.

We return to our Kissel story and the year 1910. Kissel produced two new models, the D10 and the F10. These were four-cylinder, with a 112-inch wheelbase in the former, and 124-inch in the latter. The body styles were the five and seven passenger touring, four passenger tonneau, coupe, semi-racer, and a limousine. The seating arrangement in the seven-passenger touring had the driver and passenger with two seats in the middle, and three in the rear. Held over were the LD10, 30 horsepower, four-cylinder, and the large G10 six-cylinder model now stretched over a 132 inch wheelbase.

In this year the Kissel Motor Car Company contracted with the Niagara Fire Extinguisher Company to install an automatic sprinkling system that could pump one hundred gallons per minute over an extensive duct system. Water came from a 50,000 gallon tank on a 100 foot high tower, and a 40,000 gallon tank on an 80 foot steel tower. The hope at the time was that in addition to protecting the plant from fire it would save four-fifths of the insurance premium.

The manufacturing space was further enlarged in 1910 when Kissel's Hartford Plow Works was sold to the David Bradley Company of Bradley, Illinois. The Hartford Plow Works had been in existence since 1860.

The Kissel California sales distributorship was active in publicity for its KisselKars by entering a Los Angeles to Phoenix road race. A Kissel traveled the 483 miles in 15 hours and 44 minutes, beating the old record by over three hours. Its agents were proud to point out that it defeated the likes of the Franklin, Pope Hartford, Apperson, Mercer, Maxwell, Reo, Rambler, Duncar, Ford, and Velie.

Along the same line, but a bit more ludicrous, was a KisselKar performance planned together with a Ringling Brothers circus performance in Chicago. Two circus strong men

16

sat opposite each other with a platform balanced over their knees. A KisselKar with a load of passengers rode over the platform, thus suspended.

By end of 1910 Mr. H.K. Butterfield, president of the Kissel Motor Car Company had left his position in Wisconsin as a United States district attorney and settled in California, where he remained active in the KisselKar distributorship. Surprisingly, the presidency of the company, at least nominally, remained for a time yet in his hands, although he was separated geographically from the home factory.

In the same year of 1910 there were 10,918 autos registered with the State of Wisconsin Secretary of State, as the law then required. There were 256 Wisconsin auto dealers and six motorcycle dealers. The license fee was just two dollars, with the early intent that the single payment was good as long as the vehicle remained with the original owner.

The passenger cars for 1911 continued with the four- and six-cylinder models. It presented with engine sizes of 30, 50, and 60 horsepower. There was an even larger array of body styles. These included several sizes of open touring

cars, the single seater semi-racer, and an enclosed seven-passenger limousine.

In 1911 Kissel built its first truck designed for carrying fire fighting equipment, the latter being chemicals, ladders, and water hose. It tipped the scales at 5,100 pounds. This fire truck was built for the city of Kankakee, Illinois. Other trucks were built with chassis up to three tons for general hauling, tanks, and such.

By June of 1912 Mr. H.K. Butterfield was now a Kissel Motor Car Company vice president. George A. Kissel, who had been running the company from its start, became president with little fanfare or publicity. Brother William L. Kissel, became secretary and treasurer. This officer arrangement between these two brothers was to last for the entire life of the company.

The notable body change in 1912 was that front doors were now in place, and controls

This 1911 model of the KisselKar Semi-Racer had the fuel tank in a vulnerable position behind the driver seat. This sketch by the Kissel engineering department gives vehicle dimensions including the wheelbase of 118 inches on a low slung chassis.

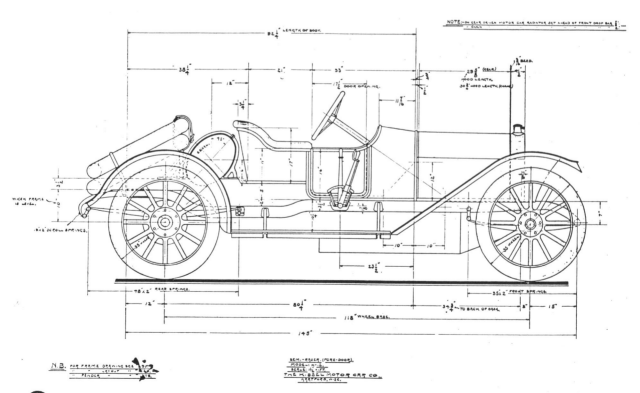

The 1911 model Semi-Racer was test driven on nearby Pike Lake over a frozen and snow-covered surface. Picture courtesy of James Grager.

that had been outside the right sided driver compartment were now brought inside the central transmission area. The vehicle designations now were 30, 40, 50, and 60, coinciding with the horsepower of the respective engines. The size of the cars ran all the way from coupe and semi-racer through five and seven-passenger touring, to the limousine for a total of 18 body styles. It certainly also called into question whether Kissel was spreading itself too thin with this diversity.

This 1912 restored KisselKar, in a touring model, was the large 6-60. The radiator medallion appears to be misplaced on the left side rather than the customary factory placed right side location.

The owner of this KisselKar in what appears to be a tourster model of open car, is deep into the innards of his vehicle. However, tire failures were the most common roadside inconvenience.

This 1912 touring car still had the driver on the right side. Bumpers were still not offered, but within a few years they became optional equipment in deluxe models, and in the mid 1920s they became standard equipment. The headlamps are carbide fueled.

Shown was a 1912 Kissel in a ¾ ton-sized commercial vehicle used as a small delivery truck.

This 1912 KisselKar truck showed the standard hauling stake body. Sizes ranged from ¾ ton up to five ton, and with a variety of hauling application in open and closed styles.

Its products were expensive, from a low of around $1,850 to a high around $4,000 for the limousine and with a median around $2,400. The production range was approximately 2,500 vehicles per year. An exception might have been in 1916 when Will Kissel, writing in 1952, recalled figures of 4,000 to 5,000 total cars and trucks for that year. This was also a time when Henry Ford, at a much lower price range, could sell hundreds of thousands of cars in a single year.

Kissel kept expanding its factory space in Hartford. By this time it was up to 300,000 square feet of space. In the fall of 1912 it purchased the Romadka Trunk Company of Milwaukee. The location of this huge factory was on Center Street, between 31st and 32nd streets and the building exists today and in relatively good condition. It occupied 200,000 square feet of space. The Chicago, Milwaukee, and St. Paul Railroad skirted the east side of this property for railroad access. This new plant was to be used only for assembly of KisselKars. Little was ever mentioned of this Milwaukee branch of manufacturing, but it was unsuccessful. The location was then felt to be advantageous in its proximity to Milwaukee suppliers such as the A.O. Smith Company for frames.

Kissel had extravagant hopes of producing 10,000 pleasure and commercial cars in a year. This never happened. But it was noted, that within the six years since its inception, the company had grown to a capitalization of one million dollars.

In 1913 Kissel offered a foot operated electric starter with a storage battery and dynamo for electric headlights and tail lights.

Mention should be made of the body designer for the Kissel Motor Car Company. This person was J. Friedrich Werner, called Fred or Fritz by his fellow workers. He was trained in the art of coach making in his native Germany. Werner was highly regarded as a scientific and ingenious body designer. He remained the Kissel body designer for the life of the company. He arrived on the Kissel scene around the same time as did Herman Palmer.

The 1913 vehicle offerings were the same but now the large 60 model had stretched to a 140-inch wheelbase. Kissel claimed as original its newly introduced double kick up frame. In actuality, Royal Tourist also had this feature. This allowed a lowered center of gravity with the kicked up or elevated front and rear chassis portions over the axles. In 1913 Kissel went to the S.A.E. system of horsepower ratings. This method earlier was called the A.L.A.M. named after the Association of Licensed Automobile Manufacturers. This formula is equated as follows, essentially: The bore of the cylinder is squared and multiplied by the number of cylinders, and then divided by 2.5, at a piston speed of 1,000 rpm's. This method was the basis in some states for calculating the auto license fees. However, much of the Kissel advertising listed the larger numbered brake horsepower values. As these values were greater than those of the S.A.E. method, it also was a more favorable comparison for the buyer who was looking at other vehicles with the horsepower shown in this manner.

A press release in October of 1913 announced a new dimmer switch for the headlamps. "At present the engineering and experimental departments are getting out a dimmer switch for the large electrical head lamps on the pleasure car models. The ray of light thrown by these lamps is too strong to be used on city streets and in some cities ordinances forbidding their use within the limits have been passed. At the same time the law requires

This 1912 frontal view of the 4-30 Semi-Racer showed the last year in which the driver's wheel was located on the right side. Owner of the vehicle at the time was Bob Nesmith, of Houston, Texas.

lights on the front of the car, and dash lights have been carried to be used when the head lights are out."

Kissel used the Motometer for its radiator temperature gauge. This also served as a radiator emblem, as it was situated right over the top of the radiator casing. A window in the gauge showed colored fluid to warn against overheating, leaky radiator, open drain cock, broken fan belt and such. This of course predated the placement of the gauge on the dash of the vehicle. The Boyce Motometer Company commented that from the driver seat you have no view into the engine compartment and with this device you could spot heating problems. This company made the point of saying that by the use of this invention and spending five to ten dollars you might save hundreds of dollars in engine repair. Some of the Kissel models had the red lettered "Kissel" written across the front glass of the Motometer.

Kissel trucks were now made in sizes all the way from 1,500 pounds, one and one-half ton, two ton, three ton, four ton, and five ton. The smaller trucks were powered by the small 30 horsepower, four-cylinder engine and the larger from three ton up by the 50 horsepower, four-cylinder engine. Kissel offered to build whatever type the customer wanted. The standard was the stake body, and they also offered the chemical and hose fire wagon, police and patrol wagons, and the KisselKar ambulance.

Kissel trucks were being looked on with favor by private and government interests. The city of Washington, D.C., bought five Kissel 1,500 pound delivery wagons to be used in their postal delivery system. They became interested in the truck after seeing it displayed in the New York Auto Show. The same year the city of Hartford purchased its first Kissel combination chemical and hose fire truck. As a further example, the city of Milwaukee purchased two KisselKar trucks to be used in their water works department.

The body plant had been operating out of a site in Hartford away from the main factory plant. In 1913, the body plant was moved away from this separate site into the main factory confines. This saved considerable hauling of bodies to the main plant and gave a new

impetus to the body factory.

By July of 1913 Kissel had 11 main factory branches. These were St. Paul, Minneapolis, Chicago, Dallas, Toledo, Boston, Kansas City, Los Angeles, Philadelphia, New York, and Milwaukee. Harry Branstetter was prominent in Chicago sales. The Pacific KisselKar branch was especially strong. Entry of the Kissel product, both passenger cars and commercial vehicles, was made into eight foreign countries, including Hawaii, New Zealand, Sweden, and Chile.

Factory records showed that more than 350 Kissel Kars were being driven by physicians and real estate dealers. This point was made by Frank J. Edwards, the KisselKar publicity manager, "The physician requires in his car the utmost dependability as well as comfort and style. The car that serves him well is the best recommended car in the world, for the physician's approving word goes a long way. We can trace many inquiries and sales of KisselKars to the good word of some M.D. who drives one.

"The real estate dealer probably demands a greater mileage from his car than the doctor, while he is just as particular as to its comforts and reliability. The time saved to him through the use of a car is an invaluable asset, but he has a deeper reason for the positive affectation with which he regards it. Any real estate man will freely acknowledge that the automobile has increased suburban land values to the extent of many millions of dollars."

"What the automobile has done to increase the efficiency of the physician is, of course, not so easily traceable in dollars and cents, but it is equally obvious. Many a life has been saved through the speedy response of the doctor's car, when, in the old horse and buggy days, it would have been impossible to reach the sufferer in time. Many doctors cover 100 to 150 miles a day on the round of calls where, with a horse, 20 miles would be about the best average possible."

The above accounting seems idyllic and a time long past, with the change to vehicle rescue squads, and hospital practice.

There was some economic down trending in 1914, but the Kissel Motor Car Company sounded all optimism, at least in their public utterances. The output of the automobile factories of America in 1913 reached a value of $500,000,000 and gave direct employment to 100,000 men according to semi official statistics. Some 25,000 cars were marketed in 1905 and by 1913 the number was 500,000 cars. All references to workers was to workmen, hands, and such descriptions. Women were employed at secretarial positions, but not in the factory production.

An interesting event in that year happened when Walter Johnson was a pitcher for the Washington baseball team. The officials of his team had his good right pitching arm insured for $100,000. They were considerably perturbed upon receipt of a photograph showing the great Walter in the act of cranking an automobile. Walter's uncle, Dr. J.H. Johnson, owned a KisselKar of a vintage prior to the adoption of self starters. Upon a visit to nephew Walter's farm near Coffeyville, Kansas the speed king essayed to crank the doctor's machine. A bystander with a camera snapped the picture and sent it to the Washington team. It was reported that the coffers of the Western Union were swelled that day by a vigorous message to Walter to take no more such chances.

Drivers were bringing back reports of high mileages in their KisselKars. A Hartford, Wisconsin photographer logged 125,000 miles in five years. A Nebraska real estate dealer put on 60,000 miles with only a valve grinding job needed. A Milwaukee contractor traveled 110,000 miles and he optimistically felt he could double this mileage. A fuel consumption of one gallon for 14 miles was a common experience, varying somewhat with speeds and conditions of travel.

A driver in Los Angeles gave very exacting records kept on his 1911 KisselKar 50. His average mileage per gallon was 16.32; a pound of grease to 842.15 miles; a set of tires for every 10,000 miles; and a set of inner tubes in 12,308 miles. He also figured or estimated that his car had depreciated $960 in three years.

It is thus apparent that the early motorist was frequently delayed and inconvenienced from tires wearing thin and also blowing out. Progress had not been made in the ingredients and construction of tires to the extent that the rest of the vehicle had achieved.

The winter of 1913-1914 was notable in the automobile industry for the greatly increased interest in closed gasoline cars. The perfection of the lighting system and many little refinements of construction did away with former annoyances and complications. Added to this, the roads were being paved and improved and entry made into former inaccessible locations.

Frank J. Edwards, publicity manager for the Kissel Motor Car Company, made some interesting observations about laymen and their understanding of automobiles. "Every season adds noticeably to the number of laymen who thoroughly understand automobiles. The type of buyer who cares to discuss technical details is still greatly in the minority as are those understanding the intricacies of mechanical construction.

"There are certain points that every prospective purchaser, novice to expert, is more concerned about and about which they must be satisfied before a sale is possible. These include the appearance of the car, its attributes of comfort and convenience, its facility of operation and the accessibility of its working parts.

"Inspecting and demonstrating the car having cleared up these questions, the wise purchaser will ask about the experiences of present owners. If the car looks well, rides well, drives well, and in addition has a record and reputation for satisfactory service, the prospect is generally convinced and it is useless to burden his mind with technicalities, over which there is at best, always possible argument. I try to convince the customer that the KisselKar is fine appearing, road worthy and simply operated, of superior riding quality, and of high standing among owners for efficient and economic service. If I fail in any of these counts I expect to lose the sale."

A.S. Robinson was the manager of the Los Angeles KisselKar branch. He also had quite a record as a race driver and he related this experience. "The funniest thing I ever saw in all my experience in racing occurred in New Jersey. There were four of us entered in a mile race which was held over a straightaway. There had been a number of other events preceding it, and when we pulled up to the starting line I noticed that the motor of one of my competitor's cars seemed to be very hot.

The water in his engine was boiling and I suggested to starter Fred Wagner that he allow the man a moment to pull over to a hydrant a little ways ahead of the starting line and take on some cool water. He consented and the driver accordingly did it. Now he was the competitor that I really feared the most. His car was an English Daimler and I knew it to be as fast as mine. He backed up to the starting line and Wagner gave us the word and we were off. All the way I kept looking out of the tail of my eye for the Daimler, but he never showed. And after I had won I discovered why. The reverse gear of the Daimler was controlled by a third lever, which it was necessary to shift before the car could be brought into the forward speeds. In the excitement of the starting moment the driver had forgotten to shift this lever after he had backed from the hydrant. When Wagner gave the word he started backwards at a tremendous rate. Needless to say this proved too heavy a handicap to overcome in a mile race. Now if I had not suggested that he be allowed to take some cool water he would not have had his reverse gear engaged and might have beaten me. I guess virtue is its own reward, sometimes anyhow."

With the large number of teams of horses on the road and on the fields there were frequent collisions between horses and cars. Other accidents of this nature were caused by horses becoming frightened and going out of control and into collision with vehicles.

The Kissel Motor Car Company was aware of the increasing use of trucks on farms, industry, and all businesses where haulage was an integral part. The truck was replacing the horse for hauling. A wholesale company of Woonsocket, Rhode Island had two trucks in service. This made possible the discarding of three horse rigs. The horses together covered 45 miles a day. But the trucks were averaging 50 miles each.

Companies that formerly used railway freight services exclusively were now also looking to the truck to move their wares with much more convenience and speed. In this year an association of railroads appealed to President Woodrow Wilson for some kind of regulatory rule to help their industry. Their presentation to President Wilson reviewed the difficulties then confronting the railroads, and recognizing an emergency, asked that the railroads be given extra revenues. The memorandum recited that the European War had resulted in general depression of business in the American continent and the dislocation of credits at home and abroad. Complaints were also made of increased operating costs because of government regulation.

Bus lines were being instituted to replace city and interurban electric train services. Many communities were in the midst of disputes over this change over.

In September of 1914 fourteen freight car loads of one and one-half ton KisselKar trucks left the plant of the Kissel Motor Car Company, their first military shipment. These were consigned to the government of Greece. This was the first installment of fifty of these vehicles, all placed by the Greek minister to the United States, Agamemnon Schleimann, with the local concern. These trucks were loaded two to a boxcar, with numerous spare parts in huge wooden boxes. It was understood that the KisselKar trucks were but a part of an entire shipment of American goods to be sent to Greece. William L. Kissel, long after retiring, recounted that this shipment was sunk by German submarines. There were a total of three Greek shipments from Kissel before the year was over. Speculation was current as to whether Greece was getting ready for war against Turkey, which in turn was declared as getting ready to join Germany and Austria-Hungary against the Triple Entente of Britain, France, and Russia.

Earlier, in late 1912, it had been mentioned that Kissel had taken over a 200,000 square foot plant in Milwaukee on Center Street, between 31st and 32nd Streets. Advertising at the time mentioned that Kissel wished it for assembly purposes for its model 6-48 and its 4-40. This was not a paying proposition for Kissel and it received very little publicity. By 1914 they were on their way out of Milwaukee. Describing this situation, the following announcement appeared in an April 1914 issue of Motor World: "The Kissel Motor Car Company of Hartford, Wisconsin is about to close its Milwaukee branch plant, established two years ago, and consolidate all of its production operations in Hartford. As a result of the conclusion of the negotiations by the West-inghouse Lamp Company of New York for the purchase of the former Romadka Trunk Works at 32nd and Center streets in Milwaukee for its new Western branch lamp manufacture, the Kissel Company found itself without a plant in Milwaukee, and inasmuch as the officers determined some time ago to consolidate operations, no further effort was made to secure local accommodations. In consequence a large addition, providing 60,000 square feet of floor space, is now being constructed in Hartford."

Newly advertised in the summer of 1914 was the two-door 48-Six KisselKar. Kissel claimed that they were following, not creating public sentiment in adopting this body. What it consisted of was a vehicle compartment with no doors in front, and with two doors for the back seat. The front seats were individual with an eight-inch aisle between them. Advertising stressed the clean lines of this arrangement, and the ease with which the occupants could mingle between the front and rear seats. All of this seems unthinkable by modern conceptions of comfort and convenience.

But Kissel claimed that this is what the public wanted. A more practical feature of this car was the centralization of all electric wires on a control panel attached to the front of the dash. It was stressed that this would ease the finding of electrical problems, and the body could be removed without cutting a wire.

Wisconsin State Governor, Francis E. McGovern, bought one of the first 1914 KisselKars, the 48-Six, for his own personal use at

This 1914 KisselKar, Model 4-40 was owned by Mrs. E. Ann Klein of Elizabethtown, Pennsylvania at the time of the picture.

This is an original photo of the 1914 KisselKar in a sedan model, with a Kissel employee at the railroad siding. This model shows the optional bumper and the hexagonal head lamps. Also evident is the motometer.

state expense. This model was new in having the long stroke of five and one half inches. This model also had the lengthened wheelbase of 142 inches.

The new KisselKar model 36 came out in late summer of 1914. Scant mention of it was already made in May of that year. This model featured something new. It was a detachable sedan top for winter use. It was added that this detachable top was a logical evolution of the successful two-door body design introduced by the Kissels with the series B 48-Six earlier in the year. This top would be optional to purchasers of some KisselKar models for the 1915 season.

The top fit snugly and perfectly over the touring body, and was so simple in construction that two inept men could make the changes with a screwdriver and a wrench. Six bolts and sockets, three on either side, and four top irons, one on each corner, were the only fastenings, and these were neatly hidden under the leather lining. The electric wiring connected automatically as the upper and lower halves met. To convert the touring car it was necessary to remove only the windshield, summer top and molding, then to screw a metal plate over the latches.

The point was made that no sacrifice was made in looks, comfort or convenience, with no unsightly obstruction appearing. The door hinges were completely concealed. The union of the upper and lower doors was accomplished by means of dowel plates, and the latch of the united doors was just above the joining point.

Removal of the detachable top revealed a touring body with individual forward seats with the eight inch aisle between. If the top for winter driving was not preferred the buyer of the "36" could have the conventional four-door body. The cost of the detachable top was $350.

In a scrapbook begun in 1952, 22 years after the demise of the Kissel Motor Car Company, Will Kissel wrote as follows in reference to the detachable top: "At this time touring cars and roadsters were 95 percent of the production of all makes of cars. The enclosed cars, sedans, coupes, limousines were for the few only as they were mostly bodies built by the custom body builders to take the place of the open or

touring cars for winter use. This meant a separate car or a complete change on the chassis and was too expensive for the average man. In 1914 we (I) got the bright idea to make a two-in-one body which would serve a double purpose for summer and winter use by removing the entire upper or glass part and frame of the sedan and replacing it with the cloth top, windshield and the moldings.

"The car was shipped to our dealers as a sedan and the cloth top, windshield, and moldings we placed in a crate. Most of the crates were never opened as most of the buyers or owners preferred the enclosed car for summer use also. This job went over big for five years until 1919 when all makers had shifted most of their production to sedans and coupes." Apparently central to this problem of manufacturing a good winter car was the inability of the industry at that early time to make a complete steel top made integral to the body of the car.

In Will Kissel's scrapbook is a small brochure about four by five inches in size. This relates the honoring of Mr. G.A. Kissel, his brother, on January 4, 1916 by the National Automobile Chamber of Commerce in New York City. The banquet was held in the venerable Waldorf Astoria Hotel. The award was described as the decoration of Mr. George A. Kissel for winning the All Year Round Prize by its awards committee. This was based on its decision for "Your delectable Perennial Top, with sound proof lighting and concealed ventilation. For more than a decade prior to your invention the greatest body laborers in the world had been laboring toward the perfection of the Permanently Closed Car. Just at the time when the Body Building branch of your industry was at its most successful and satisfactory stage you appeared upon the scene and Killed the Goose that laid the Golden Limousine. You, sir, are the Father of the Poor Man's Landaulet. You harkened to the Voice of the People, calling for the East Side Top. It was you, Mr. Kissel, who introduced the Principle of the Folding bed into modern motor construction.

"You are now in the same category with the man who invented the Dollar Watch, the Restless Film, the Fireless Cooker, the Morris Chair and the Extension Table. Had you been known a little earlier the Eden Musee might have held out longer against the waning desire of the public to view celebrities in wax. "But your ghost will always haunt the halls of Demountable Fame and the memory of your good work will rattle down through the ages, an everlasting rebuke to the man who once maintained two cars when one Kissel will do.

"You have forced nearly every manufacturer to put the lid on the Touring Car.

> In Sunshine and Blizzard we'll remember the Name
> Of the man who made Riding a Joy in the rain
> We love you in winter, we love you in the fall
> But in the Golden Summer Time, we Love you Best of All."

If all of this shower of words seems to be very poetic and in the vein of hyperbole, one could not much blame brother Will Kissel from making this comment on the bottom of this commemorative booklet honoring George A. Kissel, "My design and patent. But G.A. was president and received the decoration. I was not at the meeting."

Indeed the official patent, covering some four pages, was in the names of W.L. Kissel and J.F. Werner, their body engineer. This was for a Convertible Automobile Body, with the application filing on July 21, 1917, and the actual patent issuance years later on December 13, 1922. For whatever were the reasons for the delay in patent issuance, it might help explain the fact that many other manufacturers were quick to adopt this idea.

This factory floor picture shows completed convertible tops designed for the All Year Cars, and a few of the wood framed lower bodies.

"I wish Dad had bought an all-year car."

The Kissel patented All Year Convertible Top first appeared as an option in 1914. This remained the chief Kissel advertising feature for several years, as in this ad in Country Life of November, 1915.

The ALL-YEAR Coupé

Every Inch a Car

Kissel received favorable advertising in 1915 for its All Year Car and with the inset picture showing the All Year Coupe. The price of $1,050 for the four cylinder was the lowest ever quoted for a Kissel passenger car.

In December 1914 the Kissel Motor Car Company announced the completion of its 1915 line with the introduction of a new six, the 42-Six, to sell for $1,650. The one compartment touring body first introduced in America by this company was continued with the 42-Six, together with the conventional four-door roadster types, a new seven-passenger model with two doors for passengers and a blind door for the driver on the steering side. The Detachable Sedan, a three-passenger coupe, and a couplet body were also featured.

The motor was of the L head type, cast en bloc in the Kissel foundries, with a bore of 3⅝ inches and a stroke of 5½ inches. The valves measured 2³⁄₁₆ inches with nickel steel heads and housed with the lifters. Cylinders were sand blasted and milled on a special machine, all holes being bored at the same time to ensure perfect accuracy as well as interchangeability.

The carburetor was of a Kissel Stromberg special design. Clutch was of Kissel manufacture and was of the cone type, leather faced, with adjustable spring inserts.

Starting was by means of the successful Kissel starter, operated by a foot plunger.

Axles, both front and rear were Kissel built. The front axle was an I beam, with vanadium steel steering knuckles and arms, heat treated. The rear axle was full floating with vanadium shafts.

At this year end George A. Kissel made the observation that there were 450 automobile manufacturers in this country employing hundreds of thousands of men, mostly skilled workers, with upwards of 15,000 dealers and another 4,000 garages not selling cars. The metal, lumber, glass, rubber, oil and other manufacturers owed a very large share of **their prosperity to the automobile. At the close**

The Kissel patented "Convertible Top" made its entry in 1914 with Will Kissel and Fred Werner as co-inventors. It combined the open air feel of the touring car with the enclosed vehicle comfort with the attachable top for winter driving.

of this year Mr. George Kissel commented, "Did it ever occur to you that the motor truck is the only product of iron and steel whose mission in the European war is mercy rather than carnage? Yes, cannons, rifles, bayonets, swords, bullets, are exclusive agents of destruction and disaster. But trucks are used principally in the commissary, supply, and hospital service. It is due to these trucks that immense armies can be fed, clothed, and provisioned. It is due to them that the sick and wounded can be more quickly reached and cared for than ever before in war. Countless lives have been saved in this conflict through the superior efficiency of trucks in the ambulance corps. And when it is all over the motor truck will be used in restoration to build new roads, new cities and clearing the devastation."

The sinking of the Lusitania on May 7, 1915 off the coast of Ireland, while a British ship, strained our neutrality status in the European War, as it was called. This sinking of a ship by a German submarine and subsequent German use of submarines in shipping lanes was a further provocation to war for America in time. There was a loss of more than 100 American lives in this sinking.

There were reductions in price of the 1915 models of cars. Kissel listed what it felt were reasons for these reductions as a decreased cost of material, and the introduction of improved and labor saving machinery. It also listed more compact and less expensive organization. The Kissel Motor Car Company warned against the competitor who lowered his prices by cheapening his product. Kissel also must have been feeling the effects of its down-priced competitors in the industry. Maxwell had a bottom price of $695, Ford $460, Grant $795. These were makes also sold in or around Hartford at the time. Actually more of a competitor in the Kissel quality and size range were the Hudson six at $1,550, and the Reo six at $1,395, also locally sold. But all of these were still generous prices at a time when milk was selling for six cents a quart.

Holy Hill is a Catholic shrine, situated on a tall hill seven miles southeast of Hartford. This shrine was, and still is at the present time, the mecca for thousands of pilgrims who come annually from all over the country to pray and rest. Its location is in the geologic formation called the Kettle Moraine. These are linear strips of hills and intervening valleys carved out by the termination of the last ice age that coursed through Wisconsin. It was over these hills surrounding Hartford that all the KisselKars were test run before being sold. Each KisselKar motor was also bench tested for 15 or more hours. It was a familiar sight in and around Hartford to see Kissel mechanics driving a KisselKar for testing with only a box for a body, astride the chassis. Kissel prided itself in its precision and that it was a manufactured car rather than an assembled car, inferring that many of the cheaper cars were the latter.

Kissel made the statement, an admission being more likely, that the One Man Top was actually brought over from Europe by Alfred Langer representing the maker, Traugotte Golde, of Gera Reuss, Germany. This was in August of 1912. Mr. Langer did not at first find it easy to interest automobile manufacturers in the value of the idea. By the summer of 1914, after its introduction by Kissel for its 1915 models, the idea was also taken up by Edwards, Lyons-Atlas, Packard, Dorris, Hudson, Stevens-Durea, and Simplex.

Celebrities and sports figures owned KisselKars. Numbered among owners were Charlie Chaplin, Al Jolson, Fatty Arbuckle, and Anita King, whose exploits in a KisselKar will be recounted later. Amelia Earhart, the aviatrix, drove her 1923 model Kissel across the continent from California to Boston. The story has survived that boxing champion Jack Dempsey owned a KisselKar. In his retirement years at his New York restaurant he offered stories about his past and the KisselKar. When questioned about the Kissel story that he owned one of these vehicles, he stated that this was not the case, magazine stories to the effect that he owned one, notwithstanding. He remembered having driven in a 1925 Kissel owned by a fight promoter when he trained at Greenwood Lake, New York. In fact Dempsey could correctly remember some of the appearance features of the vehicle.

Miss Anita King, called the Paramount Girl was a Hollywood star. She added to her attraction in her upcoming play, called the Paramount Girl, by crossing the continent

Miss Anita King, a movie star, and called the Paramount Girl, was billed as the first woman to travel across the continent alone, and this in a 1915 KisselKar Touring. She left from the site of the Exposition then taking place in San Francisco and traveled to New York City.

alone in a KisselKar. Her trip was from San Francisco, California to New York City. She covered this distance in 49 days, making numerous short theater appearances along the way. To be sure she had some frightening experiences, none the least of which was getting completely lost on poorly marked highways. During her return trip to California by rail she spent a brief time in Hartford at the Kissel plant. Kissel officials were happy to host this pretty, attractively dressed young woman.

Thomas E. Edison and Henry Ford attended the Panama Pacific Exposition held in San Francisco. While there they were induced to drive a KisselKar with Henry Ford at the wheel, and this is recorded in a photograph. Others in the picture are Harvey Firestone of the Firestone Rubber Company, and W.L. Hughson, of the Pacific KisselKar branch.

The new KisselKars for 1916 were first promoted in August of 1915. The listing is given in its entirety to show the large range of products and their prices.

This photo appeared in Horseless Age, dated December 1, 1915, and taken in connection with the celebration of the Pacific-San Francisco Exposition. It showed celebrities in a KisselKar, touring model. At the wheel was Henry Ford, with Thomas Edison at his right, and together with Harvey Firestone and in the rear representatives of the Edison Company and the Pacific KisselKar branch. Picture courtesy of Ralph Dunwoodie.

1916 KISSELKAR

32 High Efficiency Four, five-passenger, four-door touring $1,050

32 High Efficiency Four, special four-passenger roadster $1,150

36 Four, five-passenger, two-door touring $1,250

36 Four roadster $1,250

42 Six, five-passenger, four-door touring $1,485

42 Six, seven-passenger, four-door touring, oversized tires....................... $1,585

42 Six, four-passenger roadster $1,650

42 Six, five-passenger, two-door deluxe touring $1,650

42 Six, seven-passenger, three-door deluxe touring with oversized tires $1,750

THE ALL-YEAR CAR

32 High Efficiency Four with Detachable Coupe Top $1,450

36 Four with Detachable Coupe Top $1,550

36 Four with Detachable Sedan Top $1,600

42 Six with Detachable Coupe Top $1,950

42 Six with Detachable Sedan Top $2,000

The All-Year convertible top was improved and offered in both a sedan and coupe. These were mounted on the special Gibraltar Touring and roadster bodies, a reinforcement of the earlier two-door compartment bodies. What in the above description Kissel referred to as four-passenger roadsters later were generally called toursters.

By 1916, Kissel models had windows that raised and lowered, in their sedan and coupe models.

Early in 1916, the Kissel Motor Car Company purchased the subdivision called Wilson Heights. This amounted to seven acres and was located immediately to the east and north of their existing factory. This brought their total acreage to 28. Building, then underway, brought their factory floor space to 12 acres or over 520,000 square feet.

Whereas, nationally there was now about a 100 percent increase in sales over the prior year in passenger car sales, the increase in trucks and commercial cars during the same period came to 400 percent. It was estimated there were a million horses in America, many of them working on farms and hauling materials. The replacement of these by motorized trucks thus required a vast increase in the production of these trucks. Buyers were favoring the one ton size as their favorite usage, followed by the two ton size.

Kissel employment at this time stood at an all time high of 1,100, still referred to by the generic word "men." There was a small scattering of women employed as secretaries. This was the peak employment except for a later brief period of war time truck production.

The French, known for their advanced concepts of luxury in coach building, were a market for the Kissel All-Year Car, comparing favorably with their French cars.

The Kissel All-Year Car was chosen as the official vehicle of the 250 year celebration of the founding of Newark, New Jersey. The vehicle was used by President Woodrow Wilson and New Jersey Governor Fiedler.

Miss Anita King, the Paramount Girl, now back in California, made a film called, "The Race." The subject of this was her cross country trip in a KisselKar.

Kissel continued to use California based hill climbing for their promotion. In San Francisco, on a street that did not allow for a running start, four men in a KisselKar made the 52 degree climb of Duncan Hill in high gear, apparently a feat not achieved by other cars in its class.

Kissel arranged for an All-Year Car Show week in September of 1916. They had a slogan promoting sales of their All-Year Car. It was "Ten drive winters, where one drove before." Since Kissel brought out this model in August of 1914, another 32 more manufacturers used the same idea. This put winter driving on a par with summer use, and allowed the factories to stay active in winters during a normally slack period of production.

Coincident with the high production of cars and trucks was the growing need for more and improved roads. The average road was still dirt scooped up from the roadsides into a road bed. This turned into an impassable quagmire when it rained hard. There was interest in Washington County, Wisconsin, which went about at this time securing one million dollars in bonding, to build 80 miles of concrete highways, with state, county and city money. Cement concrete highways were called permanent, and were then considered to be superior to the macadam surfaces at the time. A representative from the State Highway Department recommended a central nine foot concrete with four feet of gravel shoulder on each side. His argument was that the wider 15-foot highway would encourage more speeding. The local citizens wisely argued against this and won their point.

Causes of accidents in these early times frequently were the result of rutted roads causing springs and axles to break, or wheels to fracture with loss of control of the vehicle. Added to this was the fact that window glass, neither tempered or laminated, caused its share of dreadful lacerations and punctures from broken glass.

Eight more coats of finish than any other car in its class, many more bearings and bushings, an oiling system requiring but two grease cups, these and 97 other points, some exclusive and others standard, featured the new "Hundred Point Six," a new car first announced by the Kissel Motor Car Company for its 1917 offerings, already in June of 1916. In the table of points contained in the company prospectus there was the following breakdown. There were 20 points in the Kissel list for efficiency, and in a list of seven items a low scale of nine points for refinements, and with listings of points in-between for stability, simplicity, quietness, comfort and economy, all adding up to 100 points, to support their slogan of the Hundred Point Six.

Of course, this was mainly a promotional idea. The new engine was listed as a high speed Kissel built block with a bore of 3¼ inches and a stroke of five inches. It had a top speed of 55 to 60 miles an hour. In the axle, Kissel again built its own bevel gears. In addition to the usual 20 to 25 grease cups found in the average chassis, Kissel substituted oil bolts, which contained an ample oil reservoir that could be filled from a can in the ordinary way. This helped do away with one of the most tedious tasks in auto maintenance.

The wheelbase was 117 inches. The front seats were divided with corridor construction. It was given 22 steps of finish application over the 20 gauge steel.

The Town Car converted in warm weather to a victoria, the Sedan into a touring, and the Coupe into a roadster. Absent in 1917 were four-cylinder models which had been discontinued. Overall base price in 1917 was $1,095, their lowest since their earliest days.

This 1916 Touring KisselKar had just been pulled upgrade through a watery slough by a team of horses. Such gravel and mud road conditions were especially common during the spring thaws.

KisselKar trucks with sprinkler and street flusher adaptations were available by 1913. This illustration dates from approximately 1916. The water was supplied by a 1000 gallon galvanized steel tank which could produce power from the engine at 20 to 60 pounds of pressure, and cover a width of pavement from 20 to 60 feet for seven to eight city blocks.

This 1916 KisselKar Touring was posed outside the Kissel Motor Car Company with driver and attendants in their period attire.

The West Coast Pacific KisselKar branches were prominent outlets for the KisselKars. The open KisselKars had an added appeal for the California buyer in his sunny climate.

This price had to compete, though not in the same class, with the Ford, that had now sold one million cars in the last 12 years and made the claim that half the cars on the American roads were Fords.

In a less than somber note, the Kissel Motor Car Company did receive some strange requests made under the guarantee of one year given by the company. A New Jersey owner of a KisselKar asked for an adjustment under his guarantee for a new tonneau carpet to replace that eaten by moths during the first nine months of ownership. Said their parts department manager, "Though taken as a rule car owners are reasonable, there are some among them who would never be content with less than the earth wrapped in gold cloth, and this frame of mind often takes an amusing turn."

At this time there were two war fronts causing concern and need for readiness in America. These were the European and Mexican Wars. Hartford young men in the National Guard were called up and ordered to training at Camp Douglas in Wisconsin.

War tensions in America increased when the Dutch liner, "Blommersdyk" was one of the vessels sunk by the German submarine U-53, off the coast of England. It carried a consignment of All-Year Cars billed to the representative in Amsterdam, Holland.

At the time of the national presidential election in November of 1916, when Wilson was reelected, Henry Ford was quoted as saying, in defense of Woodrow Wilson,"I am a Republican, but I am for Wilson. I'm a Republican for the same reason that I have ears, I was born that way. But I'm for Wilson because I believe he can do more to enhance the prosperity and ensure peace for this nation than any other candidate. Any one who does not want peace and wants to gamble with prosperity should vote against him."

Wilson's opponent in the election was former Supreme Court Justice Charles E. Hughes, plus candidates from the Prohibition and Socialist parties. President Wilson declared in his speech of acceptance on September 2, 1916: "I am the candidate of a party, but I am above all other things an American citizen. I neither ask the favor or fear the displeasure of that small alien element among us

which puts loyalty to any foreign power before loyalty to the United States."

In the early part of 1917 the Kissel Motor Car Company was road testing its new "mystery car" in Wisconsin, and in the states of Illinois, Massachusetts, New York and California. The secrecy surrounding this new development is reminiscent of modern day secrecy and advertising for a new model of car. Kissel had the hood tightly sealed on each of these vehicles, and conveyed the impression that here was a very special, powerful engine. What it turned out to be was their Double Six 12-cylinder engine. It was no mystery that this 12-cylinder car lasted only two years on the market. This was a Weidely purchased V-12 engine. George Kissel had gone from the promotion of his All-Year Car to his All-Year Cab to the 12-cylinder idea. Actually these double sixes and the entire passenger car line up slumped in sales with the new effort expended on the trucks for the war effort soon to begin.

Kissel laced its promotional material with advice on vehicle maintenance. It gave common sense advice on careful driving such as cornering slowly to cut down on tire wear, and periodic oiling. In general it stressed that the value of the vehicle is kept up and depreciation lessened by attention to the details of auto upkeep.

In the summer of 1917 Kissel introduced its All-Year Cab. Prior to this the truck driver had to suffer in inclement weather and had his truck tied up during bitter winter months. These tops were now offered in their range of five truck sizes, from one ton to the six ton Dreadnaught. These tops were of the detachable sort introduced earlier by Kissel for their passenger cars.

In September of 1917 there was a new Kissel innovation. This was a detachable All-Year Top in which all the windows except the rear one could be raised and lowered. This appeared in the new small sedan called the Sedanlet, and in the new five passenger staggered door model. Thus, there was a door for the driver, and one on the opposite side for front and rear passengers. This failure to place sufficient doors, while seeming to have some bearing on appearance and body strength integrity, seems an oddity that would

This 1917 All Year Gibraltar Sedan was an example of the Kissel short lived experiment with the twelve cylinder engine, their double six, with the engine being of Weidley manufacture in Indianapolis, Indiana. The double six lasted into 1918. Picture courtesy of Applegate and Applegate, West Chester, PA.

not be acceptable by modern standards.

In 1917 Kissel proclaimed its accomplishments in a promotional page in the Saturday Evening Post. It listed as its foremost achievement the All-Year Car. This was the detachable top brought out in late 1914 for convenience in summer and winter driving. Next Kissel listed the following:

• The Salon body with corridor between the front seats.
• Kissel introduced double external brakes.
• Kissel introduced concealed dash lights to illuminate the instrument panel at night.
• Kissel introduced the double kick up frame, permitting a low hanging body raised over the front and read axles.
• Kissel introduced the efficient system of both foot and emergency brakes acting on the rear wheels.
• Kissel introduced two and three door touring bodies.

It was at the Kissel factory, on a KisselKar, that the soon universally employed gasoline fuel vacuum feed system was developed and perfected by the inventor, Jay Webb.

Kissel introduced the three-quarter elliptic springs, bringing to the motor car a new standard of riding comfort. This claim appears to be refuted by the scrapbook entry of Will Kissel in the early 1950s, in which he refers to other companies having this feature at the time of the Kissel claim.

Kissel was proud of its 22-coat body finish. It certainly was a lustrous finish, meant to last for the life of the car. Kissel lost no time in advertising the incident that happened in a western national park. Here a large deer was seen attacking the shiny surface of a Kissel-Kar in which it had seen its shadow.

Kissel was aware of the wife in the household when it came to making a choice for the purchase of a passenger car. Women models were featured in the auto shows, and in print advertising with the vehicles, and also wearing articles of clothing to be worn by the driver.

The publisher, William Randolph Hearst, bought a KisselKar from the Pacific Kissel-Kar branch at San Diego, Calfornia. It brought attention to the fact that people of wealth who could afford an even more opulent car picked the Kissel because they found it to be desirable. The same was true of Jess Williard, world heavyweight boxing champion, who chose a KisselKar, of the All-Year design in Louisiana while touring with the Buffalo Bill Wild West Show.

Chapter Three

World War One
and Kissel

Henry Ford accurately predicted a development that would take until late in this century to eventuate. Ford predicted that the day was coming when the automobile would be run by fuel alcohol made from vegetables.

With the development of the automobile, and especially of the truck, the need for improved roads was getting increasing attention. It was noted that the state of New York had just 7,000 miles of state highways, and of these only ten percent were concrete. Washington County in Wisconsin then had 2,795 farms. Each of these could be considered a food manufacturing factory with the need of vehicles and good roads to bring their production to market.

Wisconsin had a proposed trunk line highway bill. This was formulated by a Good Roads Association of Wisconsin issued in the capital city of Madison, Wisconsin. The bill in brief provided for the laying out of a State Trunk Highway System not to exceed 5,000 miles to interconnect every county seat in the state. This system would be laid out by the State Highway Commission after hearings in different localities. It also had specifications on connecting to communities down to 2,500 populations. Costs would be borne one-third by the Federal Government, one-third by the State of Wisconsin, and the remaining third by the local counties.

The year witnessed very serious railway traffic congestion. This, however, redounded to the benefit of the trucking industry. The truck division of the Kissel Motor Car Company commented that the truck not only was replacing the railroads to a degree, but also eliminating transfer at the receiving and destination points. Where goods sent by rail were handled four times, the same cargo sent by truck was handled but twice. This saved both time and expense.

It should be noted that in 1917 there were still 25 million horses in America. Of these, most were used in the fields and in carting goods. As against these millions there were but 150,000 trucks in America, a figure that was to change dramatically in the years to follow.

America had recently declared war on Germany, and on April 14, 1917 the local citizens in Hartford were stirred to patriotism in speeches given in town squares.

In the beginning of 1917, America still had a stance of non-involvement in the European War. "Tell the world what you are fighting for and perhaps we can all get together for peace," stated President Woodrow Wilson.

Talk of a League of Nations was renewed in the country. Organized in Independence Hall in Philadelphia on June 17, 1915 with William H. Taft, former president of the United States, as its first president, its principles were endorsed in four proposals designed to stop wars. There was nothing in the proposals to enforce the decrees by the world court. It went on to say that if the parties of a dispute are not satisfied with a decision they may then go to war and the League would not interfere. With further aggravations to our shipping at sea, and under increasing pressure from England and France to join the fray, America had broken off diplomatic relations with Germany by March of 1917.

Congress voted unanimously, and on April 3, 1917 President Woodrow Wilson formally announced a declaration of war against Germany, stating the reason as the continued submarine attacks on our shipping to England, Ireland, Western Europe, and the Mediterranean. By June, ten million men of the ages 21 to 31 were registering for a draft to secure approximately 500,000 men.

Executives, legislators, and judicial officers were exempted as were those who were engaged in an essential occupation. The largest exemption was for the claim of being needed for the care of dependents. Some of the physical requirements seemed ludicrous in that they insisted that the recruit have four molar teeth, not have flat feet, and not have a heart murmur, when it is known today that many heart murmurs are quite harmless. Also there were height restrictions in that less than five feet, four inches, and more than six feet would disqualify, presumably based on the inability of the quartermaster corp to be able to, or wish to, accommodate these sizes.

The Hartford boys, many of whom had automotive experience working at the Kissel Motor Car Company, over a hundred in number, went up to Camp Douglas in North Central Wisconsin. Here they trained and then

With the United States in a state of war with Germany, its young men were urged to enlist in the military forces. The older populace was encouraged to support the war effort by buying Liberty Bonds. The truck in the foreground was one of the 2000 manufactured by the Kissel Motor Car Company for the United States Ordnance Department.

38

were transferred to Waco, Texas, the site of Camp McArthur. Here they joined the 107th Ammmunition Train of the 32nd Division whose duty it was to carry ammunition by truck to the military front. Their previous Kissel truck experience would be used in servicing these military trucks.

In February of 1918 the transport ship Tuscania was sunk by a German submarine off the coast of Ireland. There was much loss of life, and the Hartford contingent of the 32nd Division was reported at first to be on this ship, but later this was verified to be untrue.

While all this war production work was underway there was another development taking place at the Kissel Motor Car Com-

pany. This related to work on a new roadster that was to become, at first, the Kissel Silver Special, and later the Kissel Speedster.

Conover T. Silver was the New York City area distributor for Kissel, and also for Apperson. Mr. Silver, while not in the class of a Fred Werner of the Kissel Motor Car Company in knowledge of auto body mechanics and engineering, none the less loved to see flamboyant body styling in automobiles. He was influenced by the attractive imported cars and by the custom coach makers in the Eastern United States. He imparted his ideas about styling, by sketches submitted to the Kissel, Apperson, Knight and Willys-Overland companies. His styling was most notice-

4-passenger Speedster

4-passenger Tourster

7-passenger Touring

This was the new 1918 four passenger Speedster, the original models of which were known as the Kissel Silver Specials, and in the color of chrome yellow, soon became known as the Gold Bug. The first of this production had the ornamental and non functioning exhaust ports on the hood sides. Alongside this model, with the aid of the Silver design, were the four passenger Tourster, and the seven passenger Touring.

able in the roadsters. By the middle of 1917 there was a prototype of a Kissel Silver Special. This was first to be seen in the January of 1918 auto show in New York. Here the speedster was shown in Kissel chrome yellow. There was also a four passenger tourster, and a seven passenger touring car with the Silver styling attributed to it.

The Kissel Silver Special had no doors for the single seat. You had to climb in over the low "racer sides." Will Kissel, in his memoirs, playfully described the discomfiture of the women with the hooped skirts climbing into one of these seats. Whether to keep the side walls of the car stronger or just to appear cosmetically cleaner, it sure was an impractical decision as were the outrigger seats. Here a seat on each side pulled out of the rear deck for extra passengers who had to support themselves out in the open by bracing their feet on the foot plates. They were called "suicide seats," with some subsequent suggestions of their being "mother-in-law" seats, and not to be put down, the women are calling them **"father-in-law" seats.** Another feature was

the Neville slide up steering wheel to facilitate entry by the driver.

The Milwaukee Journal had an automotive writer by the name of W.W. Rowland, and nicknamed "Brownie." He promoted the Kissel products and especially the Kissel Speedster, which in the color of chrome yellow, was affectionately named the "Gold Bug."

Brownie drove this car around the state of Wisconsin for about a month promoting this Wisconsin automotive product while he was going about also calling attention to the poor condition of its roads and the poor highway marking system and the need to improve them. At the end of his stint with this car he held a contest in his newspaper column in which he invited his readers to name the car he had just driven. The story that survives is that a young girl called it the "Gold Bug" because of its color and the shape of it reminding her of a bug. With this promotion by Brownie, the name was accepted as a slang name for the Kissel Speedster in this color.

The efforts at promotion through the use of Brownie did not stop there. Kissel used him to

Shown in greater detail is this 1918 Kissel Speedster. Kissel used the appelation of Custom Built Six for its chassis from 1918 through 1922.

race the Gold Bug against an aeroplane, as it was then called. This was done at county fairs. An aviator raced his plane against Brownie at the wheel of the Gold Bug. It was arranged to have the race end in a draw by the handicap of the plane needing to make wide turns, and so that at the end of the race both machines came storming down together at the grandstand finish line, with the Kissel doing all of its 80 miles an hour.

The continuing development of the Kissel Speedsters will be depicted in a later chapter.

The Kissel plant was putting up sizeable additions in 1918. Business was spurred with the contract for 2,000 trucks of the class B1 which Kissel received from the Ordnance Department of the United States Government. This order was one of a total of 30,000 trucks the Government placed with some 18 manufacturers.

The Kissel contract was basically a subcontract to that of the Four Wheel Drive of Clintonville, Wisconsin. The trucks that Kissel built bore the 4WD name. To supervise this order at the Kissel plant the Ordnance Department of The Government sent several inspectors, including Captain Parrott and Lieutenant Silpath, to be stationed here for the duration of the contract. Accountants were also sent. The military had Kissel make the three-ton truck, and with parts interchangeable with those of the other truck contracts. Those produced here were mostly used for ammunition carriers, and were fitted with a large metal box for this purpose. Some were sent as a bare chassis for the military to equip as needed.

Kissel had an earlier order to make a further 1,500 trucks. This order was cut short by the signing of the Armistice on November 11, 1918.

This was part of the 2000 class B military truck order to be sent to the United States Ordnance Department. Kissel sent out either the plain chassis, or it was furnished with a simple crate shaped ammunition carrier. The FWD inscribed on the radiator indicates the subcontract effort with the company of the same name in Clintonville, Wisconsin.

This was a scene from 1918, of the Kissel FWD undergoing torture endurance testing in the hilly Hartford environs, with the miltary inspectors looking on.

Armistice Day, November 11, 1918, was celebrated throughout America, and in the streets of Hartford, Wisconsin.

As indicated on the truck gas tank, this was the 2000th and last of the military order for the Kissel Motor Car Company. Armistice signing, which came rather abruptly in November of 1918, brought to a halt plans for a further manufacture of 1500 trucks by Kissel.

By the summer of 1918, at the height of the war effort, young women were hired to work as secretaries, inspectors, in the upholstery department, and later in the machine shops.

The automobile plant attracted a related industry to Hartford. This was a muffler factory known as the International Steel Products Company and it purchased and built on three and one half acres of land immediately north and adjacent to the Kissel Motor Car Company and also on the railway line. Some 50 local men bought stock in the firm to produce a muffler called the Uvee. Today this plant still exists as the International Stamping Company making the Midas Muffler. Mr. Joseph Marx guided the plant until his retirement several years ago.

The stimulus of the war effort showed in the attention given to improving the roads of the nation. The Highway Transport Committee of the Council of National Defense, of which Roy D. Chapin of Detroit was chairman, sent pathfinder cars over various routes from the central states to find the most feasible roads for sending overland the government's standardized trucks. The National Highway Association was fathering a system of 50,000 miles of national highways, which would serve the nation of 84 million people.

The Hartford press consisted of two weekly papers, the Hartford Times and the Hartford Press. Both of these papers tended to laud the accomplishments of Hartford's largest industry. Some detractors ridiculed the auto company and the papers by calling them "Kissel's Advertising Sheet." Some of this undercurrent of negative feelings persisted and was aggravated by the closure of the Kissel plant

This late 1917 into 1918 model is seen with the staggered door arrangement, with the driver's seat door at his side, and the passenger side door located between the seats for front and back seat access. This was featured with the reinforced Gibraltar body to accomodate weight of the All Year Top.

This 1918 KisselKar appealed to the professional and businessman. It was a four passenger vehicle with the reinforced Gibraltar body, the 100 Point Six chassis, and a soft top as a roadster.

This was the same vehicle, with the detachable top in place, as a coupe.

The small sedan or sedanlet was new for late 1917 into 1918. It came with the detachable All Year Top.

Finally, two open touring cars were offered in 1918, and shown was the standard touring sedan, not built for the All Year Top, again called the Hundred Point Six.

The three passenger roadster, also, was not built for the All Year Top. It could be considered the immediate precursor of the Kissel Speedster built later in this year.

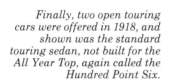

at the end of 1930 during the economic depression of this period, with the loss of jobs.

By the end of 1917 most of the young men in the military were in cantonments in the United States awaiting shipment to the East Coast, and then overseas. The Hartford contingent, in the 32nd Division, the 107th Ammunition Train, was reported as being eager to get into action. Many of these young men had worked at the Kissel Motor Car Company and were quite familiar with trucks and engines. By January of 1918, this group was on the Eastern Coast awaiting shipment overseas. In February 1918, they were in England where they were awaiting shipment to France where the fighting was taking place.

Death occurred in the local recruits from illness in camps, before any casualties happened on the fighting fronts. Streptococcal infections, meningitis, and tuberculosis all claimed lives at this time that predated definitive methods of treatment including the use of antibiotics. The influenza epidemic struck in July, leaving decimation in its wake. It was called the Spanish flu, but it did not have its origin in Spain. This was a misnomer, named after a Spaniard of rank who died of the disease.

The Kissel Motor Car Company wanted to keep its soldiers informed on what was taking place at home. Beginning in September of 1918 and every two weeks into December it published a brief newsletter called the Kisselgraph. It was headlined as "Edited and printed in Hartford by Hartford boys in the Kissel factory for Hartford boys in cantonments and overseas, fighting the righteous fight for God and country." Such was the righteous zeal existing at this time of the First World War. Later, the Kisselgraph was renewed, this time for distribution to its dealerships and sales people.

The armistice of November 11, 1918 came rather abruptly as the German nation capitulated to the onrush of fresh American troops. The Kissel plant made its trucks for the military right up to the end. Furthermore, Kissel was reported to have had 1,500 more trucks in the process of manufacture that the military did not accept after armistice. Also, the U.S. Government had scheduled another registration on September 6, 1918, some eight weeks before the armistice was signed. This included men of the ages of 18 to 45 years.

Chapter Four

Early Post-War
Adjustment

The war just over, the auto industry in 1919, and in this case the Kissel Motor Car Company, was touting the things that the motor vehicle had brought to the military front, namely through the use of its cars and trucks. And it again stressed the fact that it showed the transportation system to be in a state of disrepair and in need of extensive improvement. France was held up as a European country with much more advanced roads than ours.

Peacetime efficiency and wartime economy were stressed in the announcement by George A. Kissel of the models for 1919. This would feature a cutback to just one chassis, bearing the new slogan, Custom built Six, and a continuance of the 100 Point Six.

The new Custom Built Six had 26.33 S.A.E. horsepower, and was continued for later years as the 6-45 model, beginning in 1922 and ending in 1924. It was very slightly larger than the model 6-38 100 Point Six with its 25.35 horsepower.

The claim, "Custom Built" used by Kissel did not meet the strict criteria as connoted by the term "custom." Kissel attempted to define custom built in their sales literature as "made as if to individual order, under one roof, where uniformly high standards of workmanship govern every detail of design and construction." It then went on to list the fine points of the motor, the fine mohair upholstery, with window curtains to match. There is no doubt that the Kissel was of fine material and workmanship, as befit its price. But the Kissel was not made to individual order, although in a few instances a buyer was able to choose a special exotic interior and paint treatment. This is, today, reliably reported by the son of the former director of sales for Kissel for many years. This son, as a student, was given the enviable task of delivering some of the Kissel cars to buyers in the Midwest. He also recalls that the motors were broken in by being run on the bench for many hours, taken down and inspected for flaws and reassembled, and retested. Thus, if the broader definition of custom built was enlarged to mean extra fine, as if to order, Kissel had rightful claim to the use of the descriptive term, custom built.

Kissel was not the only company that kept a secrecy about its wartime vehicle production. This was no doubt at the insistence of the U.S. Government for national security reasons. After the war, Dodge Brothers advertised that they had contributed in the thousands for military vehicles. It further pointed out that it had manufactured some 300,000 cars during its four years existence as a manufacturer of automobiles after its long history as an engine producer for the automobile industry.

As mentioned, by mid-1918, Kissel had changed its radiator medallion from the rather Germanic sounding, "KisselKar, Every Inch a Car," to one that depicted the mythological god, Mercury.

By late 1918 the Kissel Motor Company was faced with growing anti-German sentiment due to the First World War and chose to change its Teutonic sounding KisselKar to an abbreviated Kissel. Thus it also changed its radiator medallion from KisselKar, Every Inch A Car, to one of a round emblem with a picture of the Greek messenger god, Mercury, with Kissel imprinted across it. This then remained its emblem until 1928 and the White Eagle series.

Auto accidents were becoming all too common. With the large number of open cars still in use, an accident tended to spill the occupants out of the vehicle. Also, there were a considerable number of accidents at railroad crossings. Most of the crossings had signs, but not gates or a lighted type of warning. The critics felt that nine times out of ten the fault lay with the carelessness of the driver. In general, outside of using common sense precautions, there were not integrated efforts to instruct drivers in safety precautions. In fact, licensing of the driver was just beginning to be a topic and to be introduced.

In the United States there was one car for every 18 persons. In Great Britain the figure was one car for every 225 persons. In France, in spite of their reported improved roads, there was just one car for every 400 persons. In Europe before the war the car manufacturer regarded his products as a luxury item. In America the manufacturer regarded the automobile as a utility and designed and built his products accordingly.

The Kissel Motor Car Company included this original picture of their Custom Built seven passenger Touring Sedan. Distinctive visual features were the single bar bumpers, bullet shaped head lamps, and cowl and hood ventilators.

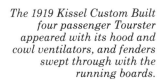

The 1919 Kissel Custom Built four passenger Tourster appeared with its hood and cowl ventilators, and fenders swept through with the running boards.

A 1919 factory illustration of the Kissel Custom Built Speedster. The reference to Silver in the earlier Kissel Silver Special has now been deleted.

This 1919 Kissel was totally hand crafted out of aluminum, except for the isinglass windows, by the Manitowoc Foundry in Wisconsin, for a trade show presentation, at the time, in Chicago. Here it was presented to the Hartford Heritage Auto Museum for display.

The Hartford boys, most of them with Kissel Motor Car Company experience, were back from the military, the majority arriving back in May of 1919. Miraculously, there was just one boy lost from his wounds, although there were deaths from illness.

Also in this year of 1919 former President William Howard Taft was lecturing about the country and in Wisconsin on the proposed League of Nations. The document was a very long one, well intentioned, but largely unworkable. On October 28, 1919 Representative Andrew Volstead introduced his Prohibition Act, the 18th Constitutional Amendment, which forbade the manufacture and selling of alcoholic beverages. This passed on January 19, 1919 and was not repealed for another 13 years until the Franklin Roosevelt administration in 1933.

By 1920 the name Silver had been dropped from the Kissel line. There was some suggestion, justified or not, that Silver was intruding too much into the autonomy of the Kissel operations. However, credit was certainly due Conover Silver and Fred Werner for designing handsome cars. In his memoirs never once did Will Kissel mention the name of Conover Silver.

With the surge of interest in the purchase of motor trucks and passenger vehicles after the war, it warranted the need for more and improved highways. This was an ongoing national activity and was felt in the state of Wisconsin and also in Washington County where, as elsewhere, bond issues were sold to the public for the purpose of road building.

Kissel made the point that almost 100 percent of the freight carried either on the railroad or by boat had first to be transported to these services by land means, and that the same was true at the terminal end to make delivery. It was evident that there was a large market for the production of motor trucks. Except for its production of trucks for the war effort, Kissel never experienced a large truck production at its plant.

Kissel expected an upturn in sales after the war. They felt that there were people who put

It was not until the summer of 1919 that the soldiers in the First World War were released from the service. This was the occasion for further civic celebrations, in this case a homecoming parade on June 5, 1919.

off buying because of the effort to conserve. People also were now buying a second car, and the use was less predicated on necessity than on enjoyment.

In the spring of 1920 the Kissel Motor Car Company was asking the public to hurry to buy their new automobiles now as there would be a scarcity of autos available in 1920. Few seemed to be able or willing to act on this advice. Those who did tended to gravitate to the cheaper cars such as the model T of Henry Ford that was running up huge sales.

With its promotion of the "custom built" concept Kissel was promoting quality, and the idea and the fact that their car was manufactured rather than just assembled. This was certainly the case for their totally custom built bodies, their motors, and the axles. The Kissel bodies had a visual appeal which was enhanced by the luxuriant 22 steps of finish treatment in primers and finish coats all hand rubbed and polished.

Kissel attempted to maintain a close liaison with its zone distributors. They developed a

policy whereby these distributors met with the Kissel management and engineers every three months. This was a two-way street. It allowed the distributor to be fully informed on the Kissel product, but also the Kissel management was able to learn about the complaints and suggestions from the dealers and their customers.

The Kissel family had a rather paternalistic relationship with the city of Hartford. Not only was it the largest employer by far in the city and in the county, but it also built a goodly share of the new homes in the community. These served to attract and house workers for the Kissel industry, but were also widely sold in the home market. This was an activity that occupied the other two brothers, Adolph and Otto, the latter having been an early vice president of the Kissel Motor Car Company. These brothers also were active in the market of buying and selling farms.

Kissel sponsored sports teams, such as baseball and bowling. Also, there was a Kissel City Club that promoted indoor and out-

50

door sports for men and women and developed a city park and tennis courts. In 1920 Kissel, together with other city leaders, built a small miniature nine-hole golf course. According to a present day golfer who was familiar with it, this course was short and not regulation size.

Kissel did not seem to be overtly anti-railroad. After all, most of the finished Kissel automobiles leaving the plant did so via the railroads. But much of the rhetoric coming out of the Kissel Plant in the year 1920 was a **comparison of what the motor car, and chiefly**

the truck, could accomplish that the railroad could not. In time it stressed more how the trucking industry could work harmoniously with the railroad business, each having their territory.

The total production of the Kissel Motor Car Company for the year 1920 was 2,446. Of this total, passenger cars production was 1,398. Truck production was 1,048. The passenger cars were Custom Built Sixes. Of the passenger cars, 856 were open and 542 were **closed.**

A 1920 Kissel Gold Bug, that has gone through a succession of owners, including Gene Husting, presently living on Long Island, New York, to the present owner, Al Koller of Washington, D.C., was pictured at the entrance of the Hartford Heritage Auto Museum. The restoration detail compares favorably to the same model in a factory picture.

The most notable mechanical invention coming out of the Kissel Motor Car Company involved improvements in the oiling system of the vehicle. Kissel engineers, Herman D. Palmer, and Joseph A. Tarkington, devised a new Automatic Oil Control, and with it a new oil basin which had a patent filing date of May 14, 1919, and patent issuance date of

February 26, 1924. The Kissel patented Automatic Oil Control worked with the throttle so that the correct amount of oil was provided according to the amount of throttle or power used. Thus, there was no danger of too little oil at fast speeds or too much oil at low speeds. In addition to economy in oil consumption it provided long bearing life and eliminated the

This is an original photo of the 1920 Kissel Custom Built Six Tourster. Picture courtesy of Applegate and Applegate, West Chester, PA.

The 1920 Kissel Custom Built Six Coupe was a four passenger enclosed vehicle at a time when about half of the auto production had swung from open to closed models. Picture courtesy of Applegate and Applegate, West Chester, PA.

This 1921 Kissel Speedster was unique in the chrome yellow color of the Gold Bug. It had an optional double impressed step plate, as opposed to the standard flat step plates.

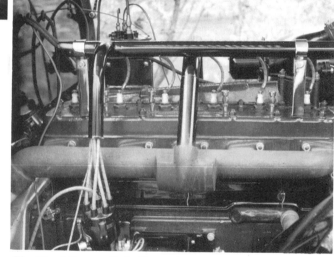

The Kissel Custom Built Six engine from a 1920 Kissel Speedster is seen from the right side. The horn is misplaced to the cylinder head from its proper mounting below on the frame. This was the 6-45 engine, although Kissel generally did not refer to it as such until 1923 and the development of its smaller 6-55 model engine.

necessity of taking up bearings. Integral to this device was a gear driven oil pump, and a control plunger working directly with the hand and foot throttle.

The oil basin had no moving parts. Rather, it had a vertically placed divider wall that separated the oil basin into two compartments, together with end plates. This prevented sloshing and accumulation of oil at either end of the pan when going up or down steep grades. Also this construction made it possible to maintain the correct amount of oil at all times in the pockets into which the connecting rods dipped.

Around the same time Kissel developed a new thermostatically controlled water jacket cooling system that maintained the water temperature between 150 and 170 degrees Fahrenheit.

Another Herman Palmer patented device was called the spring hanger. This patent was filed on December 29, 1920 and the patent was issued on May 2, 1922. The stated object of the invention was to provide a spring connection wherein side play between a spring and the adjacent members of its support might be prevented, thereby eliminating noise and excessive wear. This was managed by a manual tightening device at the end of the spring to be adjusted as needed.

Palmer also devised an improved foot brake lever several inches longer which secured not only greater brake leverage, but made the foot brake easier to operate. In addition both clutch and brake levers were equipped with hand fitted and self-lubricating bronze graphite bushings that practically eliminated looseness and rattles.

In a development intended to improve the use that Kissel trucks were put to in transporting cement and gravel materials to building sites, Herman Palmer and John Brhel devised and applied for a patent on December 5, 1921 for an apparatus that measured materials in concrete construction where large

The Kissel and Herman Palmer 1921 patented loading hopper was seen in use. The impetus for this ingenious device came from the experience of the large Kissel trucks then being used in the highway construction industry. By adjusting partition metal plates, in the hopper, correct mixtures of sand, gravel, and cement could be quickly dropped into the truck stationed below. Kissel stressed that considerable time could be saved and the truck loaded and on its way in a matter of just seconds.

Here the Kissel truck had backed into the hopper ready to receive his load. The driver had only to leave his truck to adjust the hopper plates, and then the loading lever was managed through his truck window, a procedure taking less than a minute.

quantities of materials were employed, as for example, in the construction of concrete roads. The patent was granted February 12, 1924. The general aim of the invention was to provide an apparatus by means of which the material, such as sand, gravel, or stone, and if desired, cement, could be accurately measured preliminary and incident to the operation of loading into trucks for transportation to the scene of the building operation.

Chapter Five

Post-War Recession

56

G. A. Kissel was stressing the usefulness of the motor truck for the shorter hauls, and for bringing the merchandise from the source of manufacture, or produce on the farms to the railroad for long distance shipping, and for the unloading process at the railroad terminus to carry it to the buyer and points of distribution.

With its truck production of 1,048 in 1920, this would be the largest truck building year for them with the exception of the war contract for trucks.

Sales were beginning to plummet toward the end of 1920 and with the introduction of the 1921 model year. The Milwaukee Automotive Dealers Association gave its version of why sales were so poor. It mentioned the million soldiers returning now needing jobs in the private sector that was just recovering from wartime production. The merchants and the public refused to buy, expecting or hoping for falling prices. Manufacturers slowed down production. They used the term, "buyer's strike." With the shortage of all consumer goods the prices had gone up, and the purchaser accommodated by not buying. It was not until well into 1921 that prices were being lowered to lure the buyer back into the market. Kissel, in 1920, was saying that the auto manufacturer could not reduce his auto price without reducing the quality and that the buyer realized this. Apparently the buyer did not, and in 1921, Kissel fell into line with substantial price reductions as did all the manufacturers.

The feared drop in production happened in the model year 1921 when the total was just 829 units, with a passenger car production of 506, and trucks numbering 323. Also, the pendulum was swinging in favor of the closed car, with 284 cars being such, and 222 cars being open.

This well restored 1921 Kissel touring car is owned by Chet Krause of Old Cars Weekly, and it can frequently be seen on exhibit at the Hartford Heritage Auto Museum.

This photograph of Will Kissel, secretary and treasurer of the Kissel Motor Car Company for its entire duration, was taken for a news story in January of 1921, which placed his age at 40 years.

This undated photograph of George Kissel, president of the Kissel Motor Car Company, was taken at his approximated age also of 40 years.

Kissel was attempting to sell its concept of the fine custom built car to the upscale buyer when it advertised that the Kissel would grace the Riverside Drive in New York, the Lake Shore Drive in Chicago, the Champs Elysees in Paris, and Park Lane in London.

The models offered in 1921 numbered eight. These were all on the six-cylinder chassis with 26.33 S.A.E. horsepower. These cars were all called Custom Built, as they had been starting in 1919 and would continue to be the case into 1922.

Models offered in 1921 were the two-passenger Speedster, the four-passenger Tourster, a seven-passenger Touring, a four-passenger Coupe, a six-passenger Sedan, a six-passenger Coach Sedan, and an Urban Sedan. Featured in the Urban Sedan was a vehicle top located luggage rack.

The Hartford Heritage Auto Museum has on display a two-passenger Speedster of this

year. It does have the outrigger so called "suicide seats" for additional seating for two. It qualifies as being a "Gold Bug" by having the chrome yellow color from which this designation originated. It has been donated by Beatrice Kissel Schauer and her husband Frederick Schauer, and which stands alongside a 1926 Kissel All-Year Coupe Roadster presented to the museum by Aaron Johnson. Mrs. Schauer is the daughter of Otto Kissel, one of the original founders of the Kissel Motor Car Company and its first vice president. Fred Schauer in his college days spent his summers with the Kissel Company as a driver delivering new Kissel automobiles to the Branstetter agency in Chicago. He and a partner after their deliveries would take the electric trains back to Milwaukee, and then the train accommodation from there back to Hartford.

In March of 1921 Will Kissel and Harry Branstetter, his Chicago Kissel dealer, took a

This restored 1921 Kissel Gold Bug is on display at the Hartford Heritage Auto Museum. It has been donated by its prior owners, Mrs. Beatrice Kissel Schauer, and her husband Mr. Fred Schauer. As has been the case with many restorations, it necessitated the use of portions of Kissel vehicles from different years, in this case a 1921 engine, and a 1923 body. The dating of 1921 was then arbitrarily chosen.

business trip to Havana, Cuba. They were hosted by their dealer there, Dario Silva. A picture remains showing this meeting in front of the Kissel dealership there, with imposing large pillars, and the gentlemen standing with a Rolls Royce and a Kissel Speedster. It gave some indication of the respect that Dario Silva had for the Kissel Speedster when Will Kissel commented that Silva traded his Rolls Royce and $100 in cash for the Kissel Speedster. Will penned in his memoir, "Some trade."

This was a 1921 photo taken in Havana, Cuba, of Will Kissel and Chicago Kissel dealer, Harry Branstetter with their Havana representative Dario Silvia, who offered to trade a Rolls Royce and $100 in cash for a Kissel Speedster. In a comment under the picture Will Kissel wrote, "Some Trade!"

New for 1921 was the Coach Sedan. This model was more compact than the standard sedan. It came with four doors, and finished in Kissel black, with wheels and window ledges in Hudson gray. There was also a new four-door Tourster, and a two-door Tourster in which the seats could move front and back on tracks to accomodate seating position and entry.

Unskilled labor could be gotten for 30 cents an hour. Gasoline was selling for 25 cents a gallon, having been reduced from 27 cents.

Wisconsin was considering, as did other states, the licensing of all drivers, in an attempt to control the driving privilege, and to revoke the license of drunken and reckless drivers.

While the general auto market was suffering in 1921, the auto companies were slow to reduce their prices, although they all did in time as needed to stimulate sales. Henry Ford with his Model T and his Fordson tractor continued with their heavy sales in spite of, or perhaps because of, the times. The average man who could not afford to put out large dollars bought his car in increasing numbers. In March of 1921 Ford produced 61,886 vehicles and sold to customers in the same month 87,221 vehicles.

By June of 1921 Kissel was advertising cuts in its prices of up to $500 on its larger closed models, and substantial ones on the less expensive models.

Although this was not the case with Kissel, many of the automobile manufacturers closed their plants on July 1, 1921 and planned to reopen in the Fall, in order to reduce their inventories.

Production figures remained low again in 1922. The total number of vehicles produced was 891. The passenger car production increased from 506 in 1921 to 809. However, the truck manufacture fell from 323 to just 82. The motor was the same 6-45 for 775 of them. This was the same six cylinder essentially since that of 1918 with 61 brake horsepower, or 26.33 S.A.E. rating. In the years from 1918 into 1922 Kissel sales literature refers exclusively to this six as the Custom Built Six and not 6-45 as had been the custom later. The 6-38 engine started in 1916 as a somewhat smaller size of 3½ inch bore and 5 inch stroke. This was carried over into the new Kissel Silver Specials and companion models shown at the New York Auto Show. Shortly, however, it was enlarged to the 61 horsepower with a bore of 3⁵⁄₁₆ inches and stroke of 5½ inches and which was to remain the case into 1924. At this time in 1918 the serial number began with 45, accounting for the name 6-45, and further needed to distinguish them from the model 6-55 introduced in 1922. These were smaller by virtue of a slightly smaller stroke of 5⅛ inches. Hopefully, all this detail of bores and strokes is not unduly boring to the reader but will be of some interest to the collector and restorer. Compounding the vehicle identification problem in these years is the dearth of reliable data, especially as regards their serial numbers and engine numbers. In many cases the Kissel restorer has had to face his vehicle where the serial number is lacking in the usual locations of the right forward frame member, or the left under dash placement, and the left engine mounting of the engine plate number.

Kissel was forced to cut prices in 1922 as did all the auto manufacturers. This is how Kissel explained the move to their dealers and the public: "A substantial reduction has been announced by the Kissel Motor Car Company effective immediately, upon their standard and their deluxe models, both open and closed car types.

"The cuts announced by the Kissels is not made possible by reduced manufacturing costs, and reduced inventories, as Kissels announcing their big cut last July took into consideration these determining factors, and in anticipation of what the future would offer, based their prices accordingly. The latest price concessions are really a sacrifice on the part of the manufacturers who are assuming the loss in order to assist in the stabilization of industry, to assist in pulling the grade up to normal conditions, a spirit that is very manfully expressed in the broadest sense and one that has played a very important part in increased trade in the return to better times and more normal conditions, which are now beginning to manifest themselves. In no way is the high quality of the Kissel product sacrificed to affect price reduction. On the other hand, quality and value is improved, the present models of both the standard and deluxe models being without question the best machines that have ever been produced. Incorporating as they do advanced engineering ideas, and convenience and comfort, gives the buyer full value and in a car that is unequalled in its field, at a price that is as low as a high quality machine, and incorporating the best that the market has to offer."

The standard Kissel touring car was reduced in price from $2,475 to $2,175. The standard sedan now sold for $3,175.

In the deluxe line the Tourster and Speedster were reduced from $2,975 to $2,695. The Deluxe Sedan and Coupe were dropped hundreds to $3,275 and $3,475, respectively. The upscale Coach Sedan was reduced from $4,075 to $3,775.

The Urban Sedan was also dropped to $3,775. This model of sedan had a convertible rear compartment by means of a glass partition between the front and rear seats, and this could be lowered or raised. In this manner it could be converted, so to speak, from a sedan to a private limousine effect.

The Kissel Motor Car Company in 1922 announced and put out a 17-passenger bus. It was called the Kissel "Deluxe Coach Limited." It was built much like a regular pas-

Custom Built

In a company brochure from 1922, Kissel attempted to explain what it meant by its claim for "Custom Built." It showed a worker with wood mallet and chisel at a carriage frame. It commented, "At one of our benches in the Kissel engine plant at Hartford, Wisconsin, is a man whose job it is to assemble the various parts which make up a complete connecting rod, fitting each part with delicate accuracy and adjusting each rod to perfect balance. This same man assembled the first connecting rod for the first Kissel automobile ever built, sixteen years ago. He was an experienced man then, and today he is a genuine craftsman."

The 1922 Coach Sedan featured elegance, a top carrying rack, and a price of $3,375.

The Gould Winter Top was yet another option offered in 1922 as a detachable winter enclosure for this four passenger tourster with the Custom Built Six chassis.

senger sedan by lengthening the regular 124 inch wheelbase to 202 inches. There was room for 17 passengers besides the driver. Passenger entrance was from the right side to a row of seats. There were four entry doors on the right and one on the front left for the driver. The seats and backs were upholstered in Spanish leather. The door latches to the four passenger doors were all controlled by a switch at the driver seat. All windows and the windshield could be lowered for ventilation. Power was by the regular Kissel 61 horsepower six-cylinder engine. The speed was a cautious 35 miles an hour.

The bus was warmed by the heat from the engine exhaust. There was room for a half ton of luggage to be stored on the vehicle top.

The sale of automobile licenses in Wisconsin reached 400,000 in spite of slack automobile sales. The demand for new automobiles in the United States now was two million vehicles, and one million seven hundred thousand were actually sold.

In May of 1922 Kissel announced a further round of reductions on their models, mostly of about $150. It also competed by placing on the market their lowest priced model, a five-passenger Touring at $1,850. This was the lowest that Kissel ever went with any of their models for 1922.

The body department, for the wood skeleton shown here, for the Coach Limited bus was literally a wood working factory. The customary wood used was Northern ash, but oak and other woods were used. Kissel stressed the strength of this frame by showing a full dozen workers standing on their product. Aluminum was hand paneled over the wood skeleton for this bus.

The deluxe equipment included wire wheels, and two extra wheels for side mounts, all with cord tires. Other deluxe items were bumpers front and rear, motor meter, shock absorbers front and rear, trunk rack, clock, Spanish leather upholstery in the Tourster, and distinctive plush upholstery in the closed models.

What was remarkable was the effort in time and expense that Kissel expended in testing its engines. Before any Kissel motor was

The Coach Limited, the 18 passenger bus including the driver, was manufactured by Kissel for the passenger transit trade. The Retlaw Hotel in Fond du Lac, Wisconsin, was one of the early buyers who used it as a hotel valet service. There were four convenient passenger doors, plush seating, overhead lighting, on a long wheelbase of 202 inches.

In spite of slackening sales in the post war period of 1922, Kissel still offered a diversity of four truck sizes, from one ton to five tons, and here illustrating some of the applications of the large five-ton size.

By 1922 Kissel had several years experience with the development of its All Year Cab, an extension of the idea behind the winter comfort of its All Year Car with its convertible top. In the truck version, for winter use there

(Caption continued)

were added a wind shield, and side and door windows to enclose the driver compartment. These winter attachments were available for the size range from the Ton Express to the huge five ton Heavy Duty model.

placed in any car it underwent a prolonged block test at the factory, running 15 consecutive hours, through its entire range of speeds, and under varying loads. It is true Kissel literature has listed inconsistently stated periods of block testing, such as 50 hours, but the 15 hours is probably more reasonable as coinciding with what might be run in the period of a day. Engine take down would follow, inspection for flaws, and reassembly. Then the engine on a rough chassis box would follow with a trial over the environs of Hartford and the hills of Holy Hill.

Similar precision was used in the Kissel manufacture of its crankshafts. Each shaft was tested out and balanced both at rest or statically, but also tested for balance at varying speeds that the crankshaft might be subjected to in actual use in the vehicle.

Bearings were laboriously hand scraped. Valves were hand ground and hand seated,

and the pistons hand fitted to the cylinders. The bodies were all custom made by their expert Fred Werner and his crew. The aluminum or sheet steel panels were hand hammered and molded right on. All finishing and rubbing was done by hand, and the hood was hand fitted.

Before any hood was placed on a Kissel it was first formed and hand fitted around a steel pattern, a master model of the radiator shell. This ensured that every Kissel hood fit accurately at the radiator and the cowl, and was rattle free. Kissel made generous use of rubber for reducing rattles around doors and windows, and leather between the fenders and the body.

Indicative of the financial stress of the Kissel enterprise was the advertisement which appeared in various newspapers announcing the sale for $750,000 in bonds, at 7½ percent, 15-year maturity, in denominations of from $100 to $1,000. The company did have need for additional funds later in the year when they put up a new power plant costing $100,000. This power plant was to supplant their existing heat and power generating system.

In this early post war era Washington was busy planning a national system of roads. This would encompass 180,000 miles. The Federal Highway Act specifically stated that all federal aid be spent on a connecting system of highways consisting of not more than seven percent of the total road mileage in the state, and that this system would consist of interstate or primary roads, and intercounty or secondary roads.

President Warren Harding appeared before Congress on December 8, 1922. Some of the points he made were as follows. He said that there was as much crisis facing the nation at that time as during the war itself. He blamed labor for trying to keep the wage heights gained during the war and blamed the coal and railway strikes in the same vein. He knew of no problem more important than that of transportation. Too frequently transportation failed while perishable products were turning from possible profits to great losses. He favored turning the motor truck into a railway feeder and distributor instead of a destroying competitor.

Chapter Six

Kissel Rebounds

For the 1923 model year, Kissel was preparing for the auto show being held again in January in New York City. The new models introduced were their Phaeton, an extension of the touring car, selling at the new low price of $1,485 and the new Brougham Sedan. Kissel made quite a point of wanting to bring their Phaeton under the price of $1,500. Kissel felt a need to compete in the $1,000 to $2,000 price auto market.

Offered also were the 6-45 and the smaller 6-55 now in its second year of production. Other models than the 6-45 and 6-55 Speedsters were the Tourster, the Phaeton, the Standard Sedan, the Coupe, the Brougham Sedan, the Coach Sedan, and the Deluxe Sedan.

All of these models were clad in aluminum or sheet steel over their wood frames. Aluminum was the frequent metal used for the Kissel bodies because of its non-corroding qualities in addition to its workability in the manufacturing process.

The year 1923 was a benchmark year in which Kissel and the other auto manufacturers wished to recover from their production and sales problems of the immediate post World War times.

Kissel tripled its output of cars and trucks compared to the lean post war years of 1921 and 1922. It still did not reach the production it had in 1920. In spite of considerable advertising for its trucks, production only increased from 82 in 1922 to 99 in 1923. But in 1923 the production of the 6-55 model increased to 1,676 from just 34 in their first year production of 1922. Likewise, the model 6-45 output dropped from 775 in 1922 to 348 in 1923, on their way to being phased out completely in 1924.

Will Kissel commented on the decision by Kissel to go with a car selling for less than $1,500. First of all, he concluded, that there were many more buyers for this price range than for Kissel Deluxe models. Also, Will Kissel mentioned, that Kissel dealers did not have enough customers in the $2,000 to $2,500 bracket and were consequently forced to sell other cheaper lines in order to stay in business. With the $1,485 Phaeton, Kissel hoped to have their dealers stick to just the Kissel line.

This 1923 Kissel model 6-55, in a five passenger Phaeton, is owned by Delyle Beyer of Hartford, Wisconsin. It is accurately restored. It is on display at the Hartford Heritage Auto Museum, in Hartford, Wisconsin. This had the new sized six-cylinder engine, drum headlamps, and double bar bumpers.

Amelia Earhart's
192? KISSEL "GOLDBUG"

This 1923 model of the Kissel Gold Bug was a later restoration of the wreck seen on page 74 of the formerly Amelia Earhart-owned vehicle. Earhart used her Kissel which she called her "Yellow Peril," in crossing the continent from California to Boston. It has been suggested that the peril she refers to, had more to do with her less than optimal care of the vehicle, than in the intrinsic value of the car. At the time of this picture, the car was exhibited at the Forney Historic Transportation Museum, at Fort Collins, Colorado, and this photo is also courtesy of this museum.

Then finally, many Kissel dealers and distributors asked for a return to the price range of 1916 and 1917 that produced cars in the $1,100 to $1,400 range.

It will be recalled that J.A. Tarkington joined the Kissel organization as shop superintendent way back in 1906 when Kissel took over the order for 100 KisselKars for Jos. McDuffee of Chicago, where Tarkington had been previously employed. In 1923 he started up the Tarkington Company to produce a car with this name. As reported in the Standard Catalog of America Cars, 1805-1942, the fledgling company fared poorly in Rockford, Illinois. He was aided by the Mechanics Machine Company of Rockford that supplied transmissions.

The Wisconsin legislature was contemplating assessing vehicle license taxes based on vehicle weight. The present tax at the time was a uniform $10 annually. The tax for a Kissel weighing 3,700 pounds would go up to $29.60. A Ford would be taxed $12. Of a long list of cars with prominent sales in Wisconsin, only the Packard 12 at 4,500 pounds, and the Cadillac 8 at 4,000 pounds would have been taxed more heavily than the Kissel.

With the increase in numbers of automobiles on the road the annual automobile death rate from accidents in Wisconsin increased from 21 in 1912 to 237 deaths in 1922. There were several proposed laws designed to curb motor accidents pending in the Wisconsin state legislature. These pertained to licensing drivers, stopping before railroad crossings, adequate vehicle lights, and requiring auto owners to carry liability insurance. What was not included, but which received considerable reporting, was the accident and vehicle death rate brought on by intoxicated drivers, all during this period of prohibition.

Of the 57,178 miles of improved roads in Wisconsin, 1,105 were concrete. The remainder of the roads were forms of gravel, including chert and shale, and early forms of macadam.

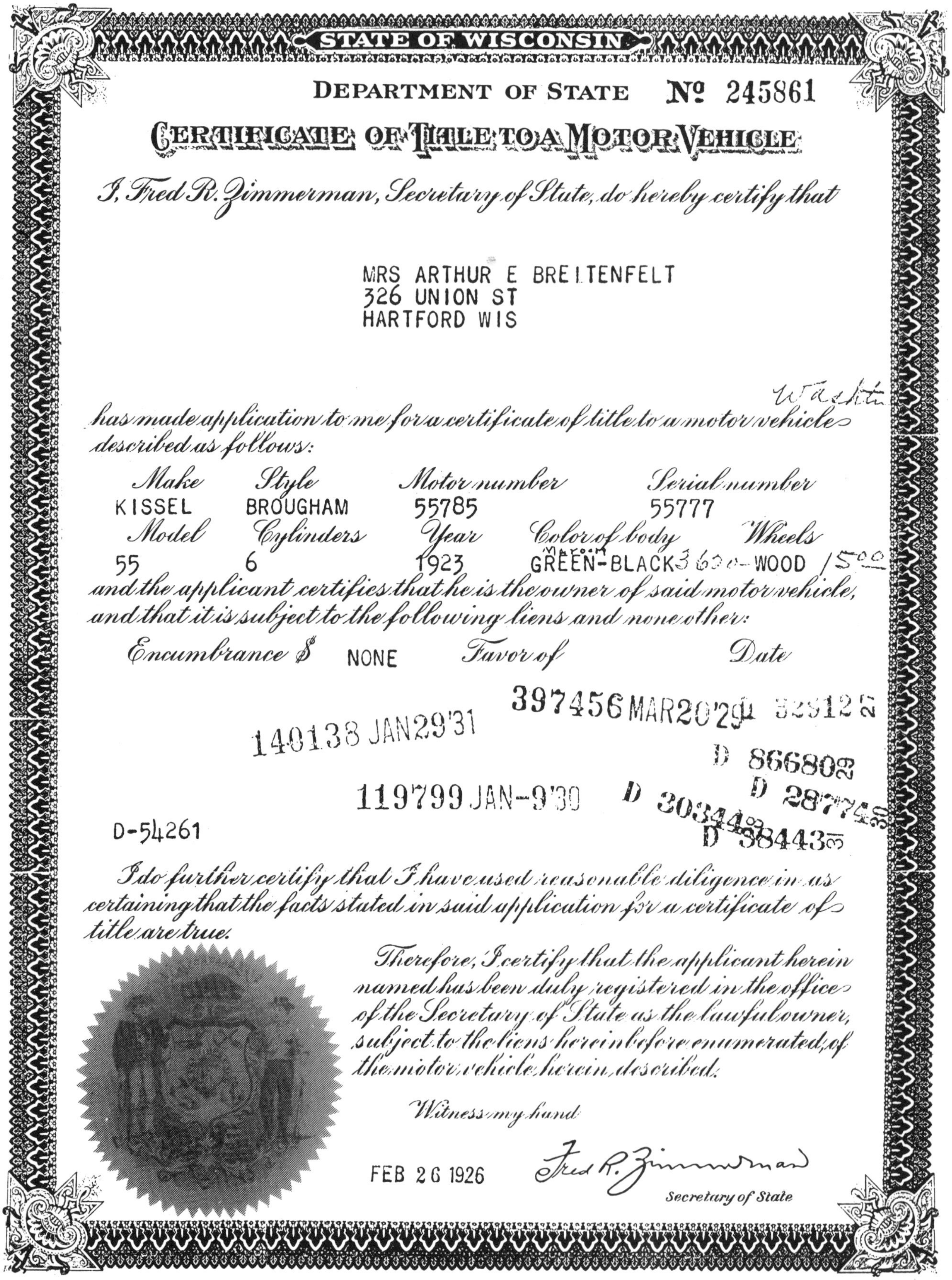

STATE OF WISCONSIN

DEPARTMENT OF STATE № 245861

CERTIFICATE OF TITLE TO A MOTOR VEHICLE

I, Fred R. Zimmerman, Secretary of State, do hereby certify that

MRS ARTHUR E BREITENFELT
326 UNION ST
HARTFORD WIS

has made application to me for a certificate of title to a motor vehicle
described as follows:

Make	Style	Motor number	Serial number
KISSEL	BROUGHAM	55785	55777

Model	Cylinders	Year	Color of body	Wheels
55	6	1923	GREEN-BLACK	WOOD

and the applicant certifies that he is the owner of said motor vehicle,
and that it is subject to the following liens and none other:

Encumbrance $ NONE *Favor of* *Date*

397456 MAR 20 '29

140138 JAN 29 '31

D 86680

119799 JAN-9 '30   D 28774

D-54261   D 98443

I do further certify that I have used reasonable diligence in as-
certaining that the facts stated in said application for a certificate of
title are true.

Therefore, I certify that the applicant herein
named has been duly registered in the office
of the Secretary of State as the lawful owner,
subject to the liens hereinbefore enumerated, of
the motor vehicle herein described.

Witness my hand

FEB 26 1926   *Fred R. Zimmerman*
Secretary of State

The Wisconsin 1923 Certificate of Title to a Vehicle was still handled through the Secretary of State, as was the case since licensing began in Wisconsin. This title was for a 1923 Kissel 6-55 Brougham Sedan, the smaller size six begun in 1922.

2 SECTIONS

12 PAGES

The Hartford Times~Press

VOL. XXXI, No. 43   THE HARTFORD TIMES—VOL. LXXI—No. 4;
THE HARTFORD PRESS—VOL. XCVII—No. 8

HARTFORD, WIS., THURSDAY, JULY 9, 1964   PHONE 673-3500

Will Kissel was seen next to the 1923 Kissel fire truck pumper in a photo taken in July of 1964 when Will was 85 years old. This fire truck is well restored, having a Wisconsin Motors engine made in Milwaukee, Wisconsin, and Pirsch fire fighting equipment. This antique is on exhibit at the Hartford Heritage Auto Museum.

Kissel added to the space devoted to building its wooden body frames by reactivating a building located away from its main factory site, that had been vacated several years before. Kissel realized that their body building was very time consuming and it was creating a bottle neck impeding the process of getting its cars through production. Kissel felt it could thus double its body output, and share in the increased sales that 1923 was experiencing.

Harry Branstetter was the Kissel dealer for the Chicago area, and was a personal friend of Will Kissel. He arrived in Chicago in 1903 from Cleveland where he had worked briefly for the Winton Automobile Company. Young Branstetter first sold Ford but added other cars including the Kissel later. He reminisced later in 1923 about the "old days" and the frequent service problems with cars. He re-

called a problem that a particular auto manufacturer had with its crankshafts bending. The factory turned a deaf ear to replacements of bent crankshafts, but asked no questions on replacing broken ones. So, Branstetter related, he had a husky mechanic wield a sledge hammer on the bent crankshafts rendering these parts into broken ones that could be replaced.

Kissel talked about a 300 percent increased production in 1923. This was true when it was compared to 1921 and 1922, but was still less than the 1920 output which still benefited from the recent European War. Also, Kissel was exclaiming that it had increased its dealership size by 50 percent since the first of the year, this being late summer. Kissel was savoring success in 1923 and was buoyant about its prospects for the future.

During a week in May of 1923 the Ford

70

Motor Company produced 39,053 cars and trucks. During the same week the Lincoln division of Ford produced 176 cars. An average week at the Kissel plant produced some 42 cars. So it can be seen that the rate of production for the more expensive vehicle lagged far behind Ford's Universal Car.

The Los Angeles Kissel distributorship was busy advertising the ability of the 1923 Kissel automobile. They had a driver take a Kissel stock machine from Los Angeles to San Francisco, using both coastal and inland routes, and making fifteen round trips, all during a period of 30 days for a total of 13,050 miles, including one round trip of 880 miles in 24 hours with only two hours of sleep for the driver, during which time the engine was kept running.

Another West Coast promotion was to run a stock Kissel car from Merced, California, to the floor of the Yosemite Valley 100 miles away.

This trip was made in high gear only, over obstacles of mud, sand, and steep grades. Kissel had the car sealed in high gear, had an observer on board, and had the vehicle examined carefully by officials at both start and finish with documenting notarizations.

As a further test of the ability of the Kissel car, aimed at its Pacific coast buyers, a Kissel climbed Baxter Hill in Los Angeles. It proved this in high gear. This hill was the graveyard of ambitious dealers who had tried to demonstrate their hill climbing ability, only to have their faith in their cars shattered. But a stock Kissel carrying full equipment and two passengers negotiated the 29 percent grade in high gear, and with the clutch pedal removed to prevent the possibility of the driver speeding up the engine by releasing the clutch.

The 1923 Kissel Touring car climbed the 29 percent grade of Baxter Street, Los Angeles, in high gear, with the clutch pedal removed.

On June 22, 1923 a stock Kissel Touring car climbed the Presidio Hill in San Francisco, in high gear, with grades ranging up to 20 degrees. This was one of a number of promotional tests performed by the Pacific coast California Kissel agencies.

The durability record for a Kissel was claimed by a dentist from Los Angeles, with a mileage of 284,000 miles, equal to eleven times the circumference of the world. He held this in a 1911 Kissel, and persuasion to the contrary from his family, the dentist promised his intention to continue to drive his old Kissel. He claimed he did all his own servicing without a garage overhaul, paying attention to timely lubrication and oil changes.

Wisconsin had reached 450,000 auto registrations in 1923. Also, Wisconsin alone had more autos registered than the entire country of France. The total number of automobiles in the world was estimated at 15 million, of which over 12 million were in the United States alone.

If America had problems with inflation after the European War it was paltry compared to what was happening in Germany. A letter was received in Milwaukee from Germany, registered. It required 475,000 marks to send it. The same letter could be mailed back to Germany for 15 cents in the United States, 5 cents for postage and 10 cents for the register. Before the war 475,000 marks were worth about $118,750 in American cash. The letter received in Milwaukee was literally covered with stamps.

The two models most heavily publicized by Kissel for 1924 were a new Berline Sedan, and a Victoria, both with the 6-55 motor. The Berline Sedan was seven passenger, with the chassis lengthened out to a 132-inch wheelbase. The interior included two auxiliary fold down seats between the front and rear seats, with a note that they fit so closely together to allow even a third passenger in the middle row.

Making it really opulent was the purchase option of a glass partition divider, between the seats, giving it a chauffeur driven appeal, which partition could be lowered if desired. This had to be one of the crowning achievements of its excellent, long time body designer, Fred Werner. While not directly involved with the mechanical details of body construction, Will Kissel had an abiding interest and input into Kissel body styling.

The new Victoria Kissel was a two-door, five-passenger vehicle, publicized as combining the cozy sociability of the coupe, with the

The double kick-up frame was here illustrated showing how this lowered the center of gravity and allowed for a lower profile vehicle, which was a distinctive Kissel feature.

roomy features of the brougham sedan. The passenger seat folded down to gain access to the rear seat. The driver's seat slid on a track in this model as did both front seats of the two-door Toursters.

Four wheel hydraulic Lockhead brakes and balloon tires, 32x6 inches, were optional on all the Kissels in 1924.

Again Kissel reviewed its accomplishments regarding durability and stamina in its California sponsored contests. These were for hill climbing in high gear in the hills of Los Angeles and San Francisco, including between city runs for speed in both high and second gears. It undoubtedly helped to sell some cars, especially where the tests were run on the West Coast. But the overall sales for 1924 were rather dismal, both for passenger cars and trucks. In 1924, Kissel production slipped to 803 vehicles. Passenger car production dropped from 2,124 in 1923 to just 748 in 1924. Furthermore, truck production dipped from 99 in 1923 to 55 in 1924. This was an industry wide condition in 1924.

George A. Kissel had the custom of expounding at quite long length on his impressions of the automobile manufacturing business, and his philosophy of where he felt the Kissel fit into this scheme.

He felt that the buyer had become more sophisticated and knowledgeable when it came to his or her choice of an automobile. He pointed out these buyers wanted a light substantial car, for general utility purposes, and were less concerned about stylish appearance, expensive equipment and refinements, that added materially to the costs, than the repeat or experienced owner. He obviously had hoped

72

The Berline-Sedan

The Victoria

The Coupe

The Phaeton

The Tourster

This picture sequence showed the range of the 1924 Kissel models. Not shown here was the 1924 Enclosed Speedster which appeared on the scene later in this year. It showed body styles from the single seater Speedster, to the intermediate sized coupe and tourster, which were available in both open and closed styles. The large vehicles were the phaeton and sedans in the Brougham, the Victoria, and the Berline sedan. The luxurious Berline Sedan was available in a chauffeur driven style with a glass partition behind the driver seat, which could be raised and lowered. Without the partition it became a seven passenger sedan with the middle row of fold down seats.

The Speedster

to reach some of these buyers with the Phaeton that had sold so well in 1923. As the members of this class became accustomed to the use of the car and the pleasure and convenience which it afforded, they became more or less dissatisfied with their first purchase and wanted something a little better.

Some 50 percent of all cars sold at the time, excluding Fords, sold in the $1,000 to $2,000 range. He recognized that a considerable portion of this group were only interested in cars selling from $1,000 to $1,500, while an almost equal portion wanted something finer, and were prepared to pay from $1,500 to $2,000 for a car. Such was to be the appeal of the Kissel Phaeton and the lower range of Kissel models. George Kissel recognized that the scope of the market for cars selling well above $2,000 was comparatively limited. This became more so as the price increased from there. However, Kissel, with their labor intensive methods of manufacture, especially in their custom built bodies, just could not serve both masters, and they were quite relegated to compete with the more expensive models. As a small independent manufacturer, they could not compete financially with the large mass producers. So the problems faced by Kissel and the other small independent manufacturers were to become ever more apparent and financially painful. Kissel was following the trend of swinging from the open car to the enclosed car, so that in 1925 Kissel produced 85 percent of its cars as enclosed vehicles.

Billed as an innovation in a sport car was the introduction in January of 1924 of its enclosed Speedster. This model was a departure from its open Speedster as being an all year car. It maintained the turtle back of its predecessor, and added the options of four wheel hydraulic brakes and balloon tires of 32x6 inch size. It was powered by the Kissel 55 Custom Built six-cylinder engine. This enclosed model was shown to the public for the first time at the Milwaukee and Chicago auto shows. While being an enclosed model, this was not a steel top nor was any Kissel through the remainder of its manufacturing days. Rather it was a weather resistant material, generally Pantasote, reinforced beneath with wooden ribs, and a cloth interior lining.

The beauty of the Kissel automobile was grasped by a Chinese auto dealer from Singapore who had come to America looking for vehicles to import. He found fulfillment in the Kissel product and had two Phaetons shipped to China via the New York port and the Panama Canal, the journey covering some 15,000 miles. It was stated at the time that the freight charges on the shipment alone would "purchase a flivver or two." But the Chinese importer had his buyers already in place.

As early as February 1924 after the successful introduction of its beautiful models to the public at the large auto shows, Kissel was predicting, hoping would be more accurate, an optimistic business outlook for 1924. Such was not to be the case. During this same time

*This 1924 Enclosed Speedster, model 6-55, **was new in this year.** Four wheel hydraulic brakes were optional on this and on all 1924 model year Kissels. Note the two **bar bumpers and the drum** headlamps.*

Ford was advertising his runabout for $265, with a starter and demountable rims at $85 extra.

The difficult year of 1924 saw the advent of the development of plans for a manufacturing plant just five miles from Hartford in the small village of Slinger, Wisconsin. It was touted as being a million dollar business, to be developed on six and one-half acres of land, and to be called the Schuler Motor Car Company. It was to build a light weight car, in competition with Ford, at a price of $295 for a roadster and $495 for a coupe. The inventor was H.E. Schuler of Milwaukee who made several prototypal vehicles which were driven successfully some 30,000 to 40,000 miles each. The plans never got off the ground and into production.

Again in 1924, ethyl gasoline was introduced to the gas pumps after an announcement a year earlier in the east. It was engineered by the General Motors Corporation and the late Harry Midgely of Evanston, Illinois. It was sold through the Standard Oil Company of Indiana. When first on the market, the ethylized fluid, as it was called, had to be mixed at the pump by an automatic mechanism of blending with regular gasoline. The claimed benefits of ethyl gas were absence of compression knock, decreased carbon in the engine, and increased power and mileage.

Numerous automobile companies were making use of runs on the Indianapolis Motor Speedway to test their cars and for obvious publicity. Such was the case with Kissel and their use of this track for runs in 1924 which were described with great credit to the Kissel firm by a consulting engineer in attendance, William G. Wall.

A Kissel automobile did very well in a 250-mile race in Los Angeles, California on November 30, 1924. This was the Ascot Gold Cup race under international road racing

This was the fate of many or most of the Kissel automobiles ever built. This sadly deteriorated Kissel Speedster rested in a field near Lincoln, Massachusetts when the photo was taken. It was later restored and is seen on page 67. It was the former Amelia Earhart vehicle.

rules promulgated by the Royal Automobile Club of Great Britain. There were ten prizes for the sum of $52,000. Kissel had only a month to prepare for this race, its efforts prompted by its Los Angeles dealership. It shortened the wheelbase on a stock car, and did some carburetion modification. Course laps were five miles, and after 15 laps the Kissel was in third place behind a Duesenberg racer and a Frontenac racer. Kissel was one of 19 cars to finish, and did so in eleventh place. Kissel had reason to be proud of the commendation given by their Los Angeles representative who concluded that had Kissel any intention earlier of entering the race, and built a special racing car for the purpose, there is no

THIS IS HOW CLARA LOOKED IN 1924
Two years later she was dubbed the "IT" Girl.

"I'd whiz down the street in my open Kissel car with seven red chow dogs to match my hair.

Los Angeles Times
5/3/53

In 1924 Clara Bow was seen as the 'It' Girl, with the caption that she drove a Kissel open car. The picture and caption appeared in the Los Angeles Times, on May 3, of 1953, with the quotation, "I'd whiz down the street in my open Kissel car with seven red chow dogs to match my hair."

question they would have won in the prize money.

Not all Kissel car deliveries were made without mishap, as witness the following account of a ship sinking with new Kissel automobiles aboard.

The steamer Lakeland sank in Lake Michigan five miles outside the Sturgeon Bay Canal on December 3, 1924. It carried perhaps a half dozen new 1925 Kissel cars and some Nash cars. The Lakeland was bound for Chicago, but put in at Sturgeon Bay the night of December 2, 1924 because of stormy weather. She headed out the next morning and when severe leaking developed her captain, McNeel, headed back for the canal. The vessel was taking water too rapidly and started to sink at the stern. The crew abandoned ship and were picked up by the Ann Arbor No. 8. Early after the sinking there were rumors that the ship was scuttled for the insurance coverage. Eventually the ship owners were exonerated in court trial.

On September 11, 1979 a salvage attempt was made by divers and by salvage workers. They used flotation tanks and a one-inch nylon rope which tore and severed at the 90-foot level after raising a vehicle which had been pulled from the ship lying in 180 feet of water on the lake bed. The vehicle floated down again and was dragged and smashed on the lake bottom. It was reattached and brought up to the surface. It turned out to be a 1924 Rollin made in Cleveland, Ohio. It so also happened that the Lakeland was built in Cleveland in 1887. It was 280 feet long with a 40-foot beam. In the process of being raised the Rollin had the body break away and only the chassis and some of the front end of the car remained and much of it in good condition. So the Lakeland and its cargo of cars remains on the bottom of Lake Michigan in a watery grave.

The Lakeland was a passenger and freight steamer during the tourist season and then continued to haul cars to lake ports until its loss in December of 1924.

The divers represented the Marine Historical Society of Milwaukee and they worked from a former PT boat named Challenge.

Chapter Seven

Diversification—
Commercial Cars and
Eight-Cylinders

The Kissel manufacturing year, 1925, marked an improvement in their sales and production picture. They manufactured 2,125 vehicles of which 2,060 were passenger cars, and 65 were trucks. This was a tripling of their 1924 output. It was virtually identical to 1923 which had followed the distressed post war years of 1921 and 1922. Yet the factory payroll, while doubled in 1925 compared to 1924, was still less than that of 1923 and even further less when compared to 1920.

The eight-cylinder Kissel was introduced in 1925 in which it manufactured 671, and 1,389 of its six-cylinder model 55. The model 55 was to have a decreasing production through 1928 when it was discontinued. The eight-cylinder was called the 8-75. Kissel was attempting, in 1925, to lure a range of buyers through its price spread of cars from $1,795 to $2,985. The $1,795 price bought the six-cylinder, five-passenger Brougham with balloon tires and four-wheel hydraulic brakes as standard equipment. The $2,985 purchased their deluxe straight-eight Brougham with a 137-inch wheelbase. In-between there was, at $1,995, a six-cylinder Brougham sedan, four-door. At $2,195 there was a straight-eight Brougham two-door, and at $2,395 Kissel offered their eight Brougham in a four-door.

Kissel was claiming prices in their enclosed models, which now were the majority of their offerings, comparable to their earlier open

This 1925 factory picture displayed the left side view of its new straight eight engine.

models. In its speedsters it produced an enclosed car and the standard open model in the color of silver gray marking the 25th year celebration of the general founding of the automobile industry. This period, of course, disregarded the early small auto production in the last decade of the preceding century.

Although Kissel implied in their advertising that they manufactured all their own engines, the eight-cylinder engine, which they

The 1925 model year brought out a new five-passenger Brougham sedan in addition to the seven-passenger Brougham, and was an attempt to compete in the $1,500 class. Also in 1925, an optional motor was available, a straight eight-cylinder, 8-75, made by the Lycoming Company.

introduced in 1925, was made by the Lycoming Manufacturing Company. The straight-eight was offered in three deluxe body styles, including a four-door Brougham Sedan, a seven-passenger Berline Sedan, and the Victoria, all on a 126-inch wheelbase. The doors were of a generous 32-inch width. The Speedsters, both open and enclosed, came with the eight-cylinder engine, in addition to the standard six-cylinder.

Kissel management was justifying itself by explaining that they had built a reputation for quality rather than quantity production. They had always been content to turn out a few high grade cars so economically that they could be sold profitably at a moderate price rather than to make a low priced product on a quantity basis. In other words, the Kissel had always been designed and constructed as the company thought its product should be built and let the cost determine the price rather than being built to meet a predetermined price.

In a company position paper published in 1925 Kissel stressed its 19 years of successful automobile building. It commented in an expanding statement, "It has seen names once famous pass into oblivion, with the hundreds of little names that have appeared and disappeared." They repeated their claim to manufacturing of automobiles rather than mere assemblers.

They laid claim to custom building their bodies, which had foundation in fact, and in building their engines. They painstakingly reworked their Lycoming Manufacturing Company purchased straight eight engines. Kissel claimed that 90 percent of every Kissel was built right in the Kissel plant.

Kissel referred to the loyalty of Kissel owners in being repeat buyers of the Kissel automobile. Some owners had done so fifteen times. Kissel concluded, "Nothing can affect the growth of Kissel. It is as permanent as the motor car."

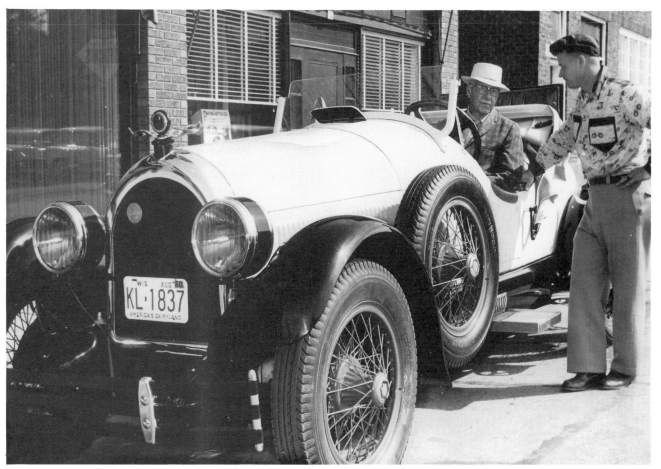

This picture taken in 1960 showed Will Kissel, now age 81 years, at the wheel of a 1925 Kissel Speedster, straight eight. Standing was Richard Braund, its owner, and restorer of Kissel and other vehicles, and manufacturer of Duesenberg replicas in Elroy, Wisconsin.

Unfortunately, the Kissel fortunes, in spite of their best intentions and efforts, saw a decline after 1925.

A trade publication, at the time, stated, "Kissel is one of those concerns that has hoed its own row for many years during which time it has continued to hold its own in the lineup of custom built car manufacturers. Located well away from most of the other manufacturers in the heart of the dairy belt, their location has proven most favorable for the business that has been built up around them."

In reporting on the New York Auto Show in January of 1925, G.A. Kissel mentioned that many prominent and wealthy people were interested in and sent in their orders for the Kissel, including a member of the Vanderbilt family.

Motor vehicle registrations in the United States reached a total of 17,591,981 at the end of 1924. Wisconsin had a total registration of 525,221, and an increase of 14.8 percent over the prior year.

Kissel diversified its product line in 1925 to include a hearse, on a 150-inch chassis. This vehicle, except for its special features, such as a wide side entry door, and a neatly finished

rear entry door, would appear on the street as a fine, large sedan. The same chassis was suitable for uses as a police patrol, small school bus, or a light chemical and fire hose car.

Also new this year was a four-passenger Speedster. This consisted of the rear deck opening up for extra passenger seating for two, thus being a rumble seat. This was offered with both a six and eight cylinder engine, and in either the open or enclosed Speedster styling.

The second instance of ownership of a Kissel by a Wisconsin governor occurred in 1925. Wisconsin Governor John J. Blaine came to the Kissel plant after he had researched what was then available. He decided on a Kissel eight, and personally drove it back to Madison.

An early version of a Kissel Limousine Hearse was manufactured beginning in 1925. It advertised an appearance similar to a large sedan, with a 150-inch wheelbase, a 40-inch rear loading door, four-wheel hydraulic brakes, and the standard six-cylinder engine.

Kissel was only second to Packard in the state of Wisconsin as its choice by the buyer in the over-$1,500 price range. This referred to the 1925 sales year.

Reflecting a growing feeling that the increases in the economy shown in 1925 would be soon leveling off, there were price cuts in the costs of gasoline amounting to two cents a gallon locally. Low test gas was selling for 21.16 cents, tax included, and high test at 24.6 cents with tax.

George Kissel was expanding on his hopes for the coming year with, "That beginning with the New York automobile show in January of 1926, we will witness a period of prosperity in the automobile business that will far surpass the splendid business that we have enjoyed this year. The lowering of motor car prices, the encouraging crop reports, the view that taxes are again to be reduced, all of these things are bound to have a stimulating effect upon business. Not only has there been a general widening of the Kissel market, but there has also been a widening of Kissel distribution. New Kissel distributors and Kissel dealers are being added in great numbers and the whole organization is growing rapidly."

From a basic engineering standpoint, three new features were placed in the new 1926 Kissel models. Kissel adopted a new, so called

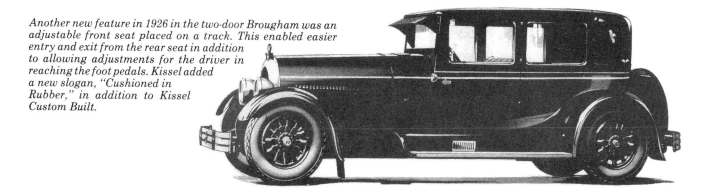

Another new feature in 1926 in the two-door Brougham was an adjustable front seat placed on a track. This enabled easier entry and exit from the rear seat in addition to allowing adjustments for the driver in reaching the foot pedals. Kissel added a new slogan, "Cushioned in Rubber," in addition to Kissel Custom Built.

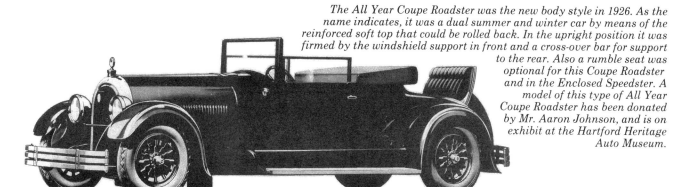

The All Year Coupe Roadster was the new body style in 1926. As the name indicates, it was a dual summer and winter car by means of the reinforced soft top that could be rolled back. In the upright position it was firmed by the windshield support in front and a cross-over bar for support to the rear. Also a rumble seat was optional for this Coupe Roadster and in the Enclosed Speedster. A model of this type of All Year Coupe Roadster has been donated by Mr. Aaron Johnson, and is on exhibit at the Hartford Heritage Auto Museum.

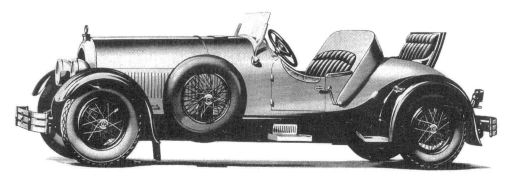

The 1926 Speedster had the option of the single seat for two passengers, or the rumble seat for four passengers. All 1926 models also had the choice of the standard six, the 6-55, or the straight eight in the 8-75.

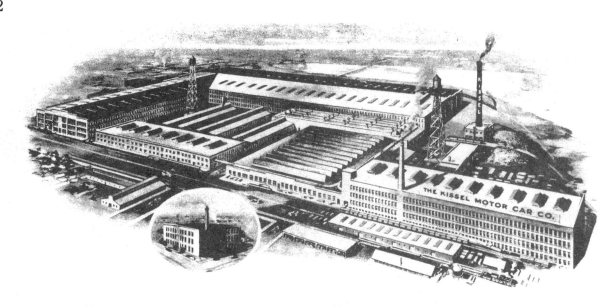

The Kissel Motor Car Company by 1926 had grown to its maximum manufacturing floor space, one million square feet. A Kissel position paper at the time noted that the company had the same two Kissel brothers as managers since their start in 1906. Kissel stock had never been available on the market. Also 97 percent of the **stock was owned by the four Kissel brothers.**

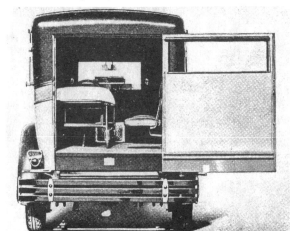

This model was the development of the Kissel Combination Hearse and Ambulance in late 1926 and just prior to its contracts with the National Casket Company.

Dual Oil Purifying System under Kingston-Coloumbe patents. This was a device about the size of a quart jar that mechanically removed sludge and grit from the motor oil. This then reduced wear on the metal parts coming into contact with this cleaner oil. The attention required of this oil cleaner was a periodic cleansing with gasoline.

The second feature added to all Kissels was a gasoline purifier, under the patented name of Gas-O-Lator. This was designed to remove dirt and water from the gasoline being fed into the carburetor. The actual filter was a piece of chamois skin.

The third feature was an early version of an air cleaner or strainer. These were first placed in their eight cylinder cars and then added to the sixes, also.

None of the above were of Kissel design. Kissel offered to have these improvements placed by their dealers into previous models at a small cost.

The price lowering just mentioned amounted to $200 a car for the new Kissel models, and that with the new features added. George Kissel attributed some of his perceived success in sales to foreign countries to his lower production costs, making it competitive, where, as he stated, custom building was more the rule than the exception. These foreign countries were England, Germany, Belgium, Holland, and Spain as the principal European markets. Elsewhere they were South American countries and Australia.

There were two ways, essentially, that the finished Kissel car would leave the factory. The commonest was to have it loaded onto and shipped via railroad cars. This method, however, entailed frequent delays in deliveries because of strikes, and other inconsistencies caused by this mode of delivery. Eager buyers and dealers were often rewarded by having their new Kissel automobiles driven right to them. It was a common practice for officials of the Kissel organization to have their college-age children drive these cars to their destinations and use public transportation for the return jaunt. Also, many Kissel buyers came straight to the plant to pick up their new car as did several state of Wisconsin governors. Then dealers would come to the factory, with other drivers, if needed, to drive

their purchases back to their dealerships and the customer.

The 1926 Kissel model year expected to get a big boost with the introduction of their All-Year Coupe-Roadster. These came in both a two- and four-passenger configuration. The latter was the result of the rear deck having a seat for two as a rumble seat. Both the two and four passenger creations allowed the top to be folded down and neatly stored in the rear. Also, side windows could be cranked up and down to act as windscreens. The tops could be taken down quickly, actually in seven seconds by trained factory hands, and quickly enough by the owner. These models came in both the six and eight-cylinder engine sizes. These were the main models that they took to the auto shows together with their earlier standards.

The reports came back that these cars were well received in New York and Chicago. Kissel prided itself with presenting body styles that were two years ahead of the rest of the market Within a year the All-Year Coupe-Roadster, Kissel claimed, was copied by some 20 other manufacturers, as convertible coupes, which had suddenly become popular after having lagged since the teens.

This was the 26th year of the New York Auto Show. The Kissel brothers, George and Will, always came back from the New York Show with renewed enthusiasm and perennial hopes for a big year. It turned out that 1926 was a good year, nearly on a par with 1925, but not up to their extravagant hopes. The success that the year experienced was due mainly to high sales the first part of the year, but which dropped rapidly later in the year.

Whereas Kissel would advertise their cars as being able to cruise for hours at 60 to 65 miles an hour without damage to the engine, this was not the speed that was reported and looked on with favor by the state of Wisconsin. After two years of study and survey the Wisconsin State Automobile Association came to the decision to advocate an increase in the speed limit to 35 miles an hour in the open country. It remarked that checking on scores of highways in the state clearly indicated that the average motorist traveled at a speed of 35 miles an hour in the open country and where road conditions permitted such a speed.

Kissel was claiming priority for its All-Year Coupe-Roadster and also the fact that the front seats were set on a sliding track in their two-door sedan models. This allowed easier entry into the rear seat.

In June of 1926 Kissel was announcing that their sales to that point were 40 percent higher than the similar period in 1925. The hard figures did not, however, bear out their high hopes as they ended up by manufacturing 1,972 vehicles in 1926 compared to 2,125 in 1925. Of this output the figures show 1,901 passenger cars and 71 trucks were built. These proportions were essentially the same as in 1925. This translates to 27 passenger cars to every commercial car built. Succeeding years were to show this proportion change to between three and four passenger cars for every commercial car built.

The truck chassis were now commercial trucks, fire trucks, and specialty vehicles, such as a new style truck built for a milk hauler. This had a glass lined and insulated structure much like a Thermos jug which ensured constancy in the temperature of the milk in transit and a lessened chance of proliferation of bacteria.

Kissel in 1926 announced the development of the all units cushioned in rubber concept. These rubber cushions were interposed where needed for cushioning against vibration and rattles, such as the motor mountings, at the springs instead of shackles, the gas tank, and the steering gear mounting.

Kissel furthermore commented on their vehicles having a very low center of gravity due to their double kick up frames. Thus, the Coupe-Roadster stood only 68 inches from ground to the top of the closed car. The motor was also slightly tilted in the straight-eight so that crankshaft and drive shaft were all in a straight line.

An interesting trip was recorded in September of 1926 using a Kissel automobile. A Milwaukee driver covered 2,846 miles on a trip from Milwaukee to Los Angeles through a southern route. The present day mileage of this trip at 2,150 miles on interstate highways is a big improvement over the more circuitous routes existing in 1926. He was able to average 46½ miles an hour and he consumed one gallon of gasoline in 18 miles of driving in the eight-cylinder Kissel. His oil consumption came to one quart in 106 miles of driving, making the necessity for adding oil almost as constant as the need for fuel. He averaged one tire problem in 570 miles, although he traveled over some very rough roads and the need for tire repairs was much better on firm pavement.

Kissel was clinging to their custom built bodies with a wooden frame. This was very labor intensive, and reflected itself in the cost of their vehicle. Here in Wisconsin, this practice was also in existence at the Nash plant in Kenosha. As a point of comparison, Essex of the Hudson line, and Dodge were making all steel bodies on an assembly line basis. Also, Buick had what they called their Unified Line concept for an assembly line. They advertised that this allowed them to put out 1,100 cars in a single day with just 900 men, which brought the cost of making one Buick body to that of the cost of the labor of one man in a day.

The fertile brain of the Kissel head chassis engineer, Herman Palmer, came up with yet another original idea for which he was granted a patent, which he had actually applied for two years prior. That was for a tire carrier for its truck lines. This was placed in the rear of the truck under the floor in its own separate compartment. Here two spare truck tires could be stored away safely, in a dust-free space, similar to the arrangement in many modern day vehicles.

George Kissel was predicting a good year in 1927. He based this optimism on the fact of lower federal taxes, heavy bank deposits, and high tariffs to protect our farmers and industries, plus the added distribution points that Kissel opened up both in America and abroad, chiefly in Europe and South America.

With the onset of the national auto shows Kissel was again sounding buoyant in its hopes for a substantial 1927 model year. It would be difficult to determine how much was in the real world of reality on the part of the Kissel pronouncements, and to what degree it was pure promotion to keep up the spirits for a buying mood in the public and their dealers and distributors. But, if 1926 was a down-year in sales, 1927 was even worse. In fact, Kissel was not to regain any of its earlier success in sales although it continued to command a

Displayed in this factory picture was the new All Year Brougham Sedan, billed as two cars in one, and following the concept of the earlier introduced All Year Coupe Roadster.

high degree of respect from the connoisseur of fine automobiles.

What was new for 1927 was a smaller six, the model 70. This model was down-sized to 185 cubic inch displacement, and a wheelbase of 117 inches. It combined good performance with improved fuel economy. The smaller straight-eight was called model 80, with 247 cubic inch displacement, and the standard straight-eight, now model 90 had 287 cubic inch displacement, with chassis wheelbases of 131 and 139 inches.

Kissel added to its concept of the All-Year Car introduced in 1926 by applying this to a new sedan called the All-Year Brougham. This sedan found summer use with the top folded down and back, and when up as a cold weather car. All windows could be raised and lowered for summer wind protection. It was offered in both a six- and eight-cylinder at prices ranging from $2,295 to $2,795.

Also new in 1927 was a larger seven-passenger sedan which in the deluxe model sported a 139-inch wheelbase.

The 1927 Seven-Passenger Sedan was the ulimate in Kissel size and luxury.

The Speedster in 1927 was now offered with the option of a rumble seat. This was the last substantial change in the Speedster, following the Enclosed Speedster offered in 1924.

This was the 1927 Kissel Sedan as it appeared at the time, showing its massive low appearance, its cathedral vault shaped radiator, and the large Ilco Ryan headlamps.

The interior of this 1926 Kissel Sedan showed the instrument cluster positioned under the walnut dash and the plush Chase Velmo mohair upholstery.

All told, Kissel again put out a rather mind boggling array of new and previously standard body styles. This certainly gave the buying public a large choice, though at the cost of the slow and very tedious process of custom building all these bodies with their wooden frames. In these early days before the advanced market studies of today, Kissel would have done well to be better informed of what the public was willing to buy.

Certainly Kissel had input from its dealers and distributors through regular meetings with them. Whatever Kissel did right, it also survived beyond what most small independent manufacturers were able to achieve in longevity. In fact, it was the second longest

This close-up view of the Kissel instrument cluster showed the easy reading dials and the fine decorative work of the background including the Kissel name inscription.

lived auto manufacturer in the state of Wisconsin, being eclipsed only by what was earlier Rambler, Nash, and later the American Motors Company, and for a short period, Chrysler.

In 1927 Kissel placed more emphasis on its commercial car department. This included their standard line of trucks, but also an **increasing production of their hearse and** ambulance combinations. Kissel had some substantial sales of these in Minneapolis and Oklahoma. But its most promising order came from the National Casket Company of Boston. Kissel claimed a contract of one and one-half million dollars worth of hearse ambulances. The vehicle was called the National Kissel Hearse. These hearses sold for around $4,000 **or over depending on equipment included.**

This 1927 Kissel Hearse was a model that preceded its hearse affiliation with the National Casket Company. Photograph courtesy of Applegate and Applegate.

Actually, Kissel made a small number of hearses as early as in 1925. The number made in 1927 stood at 76, and most of these sold through the National Casket Company, although there were a number of other individual sales. Kissel made around 500 funeral cars before it ceased operations in 1930.

Kissel continued to sound optimistic by declaring that its inventories of unsold cars was low, and it felt that it was giving more steady employment to its workers than the average automobile manufacturer.

Kissel rounded out its 1927 sales year with a production of 1,021 passenger cars, which was a substantial drop from the 1,701 of the prior year. It raised its production of commercial cars from 71 in 1926 to 126 in 1927. Its manufacture of hearse ambulances helped this figure.

Kissel, in its attempt to regain business, was rapidly changing engine number designations even when there was scant change in the yearly turn over. Kissel also went to a new overall vehicle name in 1928, the White Eagle Series. For reasons that are not apparent, they limited the name of White Eagle models to their deluxe eight-cylinder series. Also, Kissel preferred the nomenclature of Kissel White Eagle, when in the next year they shortened it to simply White Eagle. Held over from 1927 were the standard 6-55, the smaller 6-70, the smaller eights, the 8-80-S and 8-80, and the standard eight, the 8-90. The top of the line 8-90's were their Deluxe models. The temperature gauge was now on the dashboard. A three-pound eagle with outspread wings was below the radiator cap. The Kissel Motor Car Company was frantically trying to offer the public a continuing large variety of vehicle choices, while concentrating most of their efforts now on the commercial vehicle market, in their case, the hearse and ambulance business.

With its contract with the National Casket Company, Kissel was underway in the production of funeral cars. Actually these were, for the most part, hearse ambulances. Kissel made a variety of sizes and price models for the funeral industry.

There was the top of the line, model 90-B, with 162-inch wheelbase and with a casket compartment approached through the rear through a 40-inch door. The loading platform was low to the ground, with rollers to facilitate the operation. It was plush with Spanish leather or silk mohair. With some modifica-

The 1928 National Kissel Hearse Ambulance is shown in its ambulance conversion. For both this and the hearse use, entry could be gained from the side through the pillarless construction or pillars which could be removed. It also had the wide rear door.

tion it could alternate to use as an ambulance. The latter use would hold a patient cot or litter, with a side wall cabinet for a heater, medicine chest, and Thermos bottle. Such was the primitive state of the art as regards care of the ambulance car victim.

The third use of this model was as a funeral limousine to carry the pallbearers and such. This was on a shorter wheelbase of 137 inches, seating eight passengers, and having middle row fold down seats.

The next model down in size was the 80-B with 95 horsepower and a 156-inch wheelbase. This casket bearing funeral car could also be modified with ambulance equipment at a nominal extra charge. Again, this model 80-B was available as a straight ambulance. This interior could accommodate a front driver seat for three, a space for a full-sized cot or stretcher, and chairs for two attendants.

Then there was a National-Kissel service car, Model 74-BC, both capable of handling burial cases or vaults, or funeral paraphernalia including flowers.

There was a model 74-B, a casket bearing vehicle at a lesser price with a 152-inch wheelbase. This was also available with side doors allowing side entrance of the casket, in addition to the rear and called the Three Way Loading Car.

The bottom of the funeral car line was the model 54-B, for a smaller funeral operation and lower cost outlay. This was a six-cylinder vehicle, whereas, most of the above were eight-cylinder size. This model had the additional feature of being able to remove the side door posts to make it a Three-Way Loader.

All of this illustrates the extent to which Kissel went to accommodate this specific market, and its attempts to find a new market for its products. It offered a rather remarkable range of service to the funeral director through its combination of model sizes and body designs. This was all made possible through the painstaking care and engineering skills of Fred Werner and his artisan crew of body designers and craftsmen.

Starting in 1925 Kissel tended to have bumpers on all its vehicles instead of just a deluxe optional feature. Confusing was the year and order in which their cars had the two or three bar bumpers. Generally, the larger cars, and especially the eight-cylinder ones had the three bar, and the sixes and the smaller bodies had the two bar. But again, this was not always the case at least when it came to the Speedsters. Kissel went from the tubular bumper styles in its passenger cars to bar bumpers after 1922. This seemingly small detail has been of significance, however, to the Kissel vehicle restorer, who has used this information and other mechanical details for vehicle year identification especially when vehicle serial numbers were lost on the car and perhaps incorrect in the auto literature.

The total production for 1928 was 1,069 veh-

This Model 95, five-passenger Brougham Sedan was the first year that Kissel used the new vehicle name, the White Eagle. Kissel aficionados make the point that these were Kissel White Eagles and in the next year, 1929 the Kissel portion of the name was dropped. To confuse the issue further, Kissel factory literature in early 1928 refers to their six and smaller eights and the standard 8-90 as Kissel Custom Built Models, and the long wheel base 8-90 in the deluxe as White Eagle Models.

icles, down very slightly from the 1,147 of 1927. The number of passenger cars was down to 848, from 1,021 of 1927. Commercial car and truck production was 221, up from 126 in 1927. This was due mostly to its increased production of their Kissel National hearse vehicles.

What Kissel stressed in the way of promotion for 1928 was its down sloped front roof line which was intended to alleviate the need for a sun visor. This feature was further enhanced by a vertical ledge coming down from the front roof line amounting to several more inches. The down-sloped roof, however, reduced somewhat the head space for the front seat occupants, although it certainly remained very adequate. Ilco Ryan headlights were standard for all models. Again, the other Kissel features were reiterated, such as the engine and springs cushioned in rubber.

Kissel took credit for being the first auto manufacturer to feature an All-Year Brougham in 1927. It commented that the New York Auto Show in 1928 revealed many other cars now with the same feature. The most consistent claim by Kissel through the years, was in fact, that it pioneered more new automobiles styles than any other manufacturer. To question and actually prove this contention would be a moot point. While the preponderance of such a large number of body styles, especially in such a relatively small company, was a fact, it was also true that critics pointed to this diversity as one of the causes of its eventual financial collapse. But then, with their basic wooden body frame and the work this involved, it probably made little difference in being able to fashion the Kissel body in this diversity of styles. At any rate Kissel was, and will be, remembered for its beautiful car designs, for which it continued to advertise as the "custom built" car. Predominantly hand built would have been closer to the fact.

It was a beauty that did not escape the attention of the famous illustrating artist, James Montgomery Flagg, who in this year purchased his sixth Kissel. And his automobile was truly custom built to the extent that he ordered it and had it delivered in deep lavender exterior, snow white wheels, and beautifully contrasting tan top. As earlier mentioned, numerous Hollywood and sports and entertainment figures owned Kissels, but none were as devoted to the Kissel as was James Flagg.

The cheapest six-cylinder Kissel sold for $1,495, and the largest eight-cylinder sold for $3,885 f.o.b. factory. Competing in the Hartford area at the time were cheaper cars such as Ford, Chevrolet, and Plymouth. The Oakland "All American" offered through Pontiac, and the Hudson and Nash ran in the lower range of the Kissel offerings.

In April of 1928 Kissel was still battling in the courts with the War Department over its financial rewards for its 1918 World War One military contract. The amount that the Kissel Motor Car Company was suing for was substantial, being $91,244.50. This went to the U.S. Court of Appeals. The War Department held up final settlement on a technical interpretation of the contract different than was understood by the Kissel Company and its advisors. Preceding decisions had been made by the Chicago Claims Board, the War Adjusting Board in Washington, and the U.S. Department of Justice in Washington, before the final decision mentioned above. Thus, it was ten years in settlement since the Kissel military truck manufacture occurred in 1918.

Kissel had its adherents through its sales representation in Germany, Romania, Norway, Sweden, Greece, Canada, Central America, and Brazil and Argentina in South America. Beauty contests for cars was a fad at the time and such were recorded in Berlin, Germany. Here the large Kissels competed well earning second place in one contest, edged out by a Rolls Royce, worth many times the price of a Kissel.

England paid honor to the Kissel in an article in a motor magazine called "Modern Progress," under the heading of "Motor Car Industry in America." The author of the article lauded the quality of work put into the Kissel. He commented, "In the world of autodom, the Kissel Motor Car Company has a fairly established reputation as something quite apart from the regular run of production. Practically all firms aim to achieve such individuality but few succeed. The ability to build a really superior car is something in the nature of a gift. In any case, the Kissel Motor Car Company has some remarkably fine work to their credit. These new models are a delight to the eye with their beautiful lines and coach work, and have been hailed as an epochal achievement in automobile history. Never before in a single line of automobile has there been such an amazing array of major mechanical engineering, style and comfort improvements." The source of the article does not specify the origin of its author, whether an English dealer in Kissels or whatever. It stands, however, as a strong endorsement for a fine automobile from a country that made the Rolls Royce and other fine automobiles.

With the summer of 1928 came hopes of a large development to supply Kissel built taxicabs. Former officials of the Yellow Cab Company of Chicago were developing their ideas for the formation of a new taxicab manufacturing company. These people gathered around a Mr. H. C. Bradfield and his Bradfield Motors Company. The new cab to be manufactured by the Kissel Motor Car Company was to be called the Bradfield taxicab. Kissel was hoping to double their business with this new work. Also, Kissel felt that these businessmen, long associated with the taxicab industry, were also long on business acumen. This was true. It was also true that Bradfield arranged adequate capitalization through sale of stock. The business office was to be in Chicago, with branch offices mainly in Milwaukee, and all production to be at the Kissel plant in Hartford, Wisconsin. In July of 1928 Kissel was excitedly talking about pro-

duction being underway within sixty days. This new taxicab development, together with their existing contracts with the National Casket Company for hearse ambulances, was their hoped for remedy for their flagging passenger car sales.

The officers of the Bradfield Motors development had ties not only to the Yellow Cab Company of Chicago, but also to the taxicab division of the Yellow Truck and Coach Manufacturing Company, a subsidiary of the General Motors Company. Mr. George B. Daubner, a vice president of Bradfield Motors, and earlier the chief engineer of the General Motors taxicab division, and before that chief engineer for the Chicago Yellow Cab taxicab industry, came to Hartford with his family in 1928 to help guide the manufacture of the new Bradfield taxicabs.

Rounding out the professional acquisition by the Kissel Motor Car Company, in addition to Mr. George Daubner, were Mr. B.M. Seymour, as sales manager, with his experience as manager of the New York branch of the General Motors Truck Company, and also earlier Yellow Cab Company experience. There was essentially the same experience background for Mr. Elmer G. Knox as factory manager.

In addition to the front roof line change in the 1928 passenger cars was the elimination of the individual or bicycle type of fender in favor of the full fenders giving a longer, fluid line. Also, the hood gave a wider and lower appearance. The interiors were impressive with solid walnut door strips with inlaid pat-

The Bradfield taxicabs were introduced in 1928 as the 67-B model, with the same engine as was in the 6-55, and with the option of a smaller vehicle, the 57-B with the small six-cylinder engine as was in the 6-70. Both enclosed models, and those with a retractible soft top in front for the driver, were offered.

terns of wood of contrasting colors and an instrument panel of solid walnut, hand fitted and polished, arm straps and arm rests, vanity cases, and cigar lighters. The seating materials were mohair, leather for the open vehicles, and top quality silk plush for the deluxe models.

The 1929 models were all White Eagles. The series was reduced to three basic models. There was a new model 8-126 which stood for 126 horsepower, had a top speed of 100 miles an hour, and wheelbases of 132 and 139 inches. The model 8-95 was a continuation of the smaller 8-80 with the same wheelbase of 125 inches. Then there was the six-cylinder model 6-73, a successor to the smaller six of the preceding year, then called the 6-70. Again there was a dazzling array of body styles, eight alone in the model 8-126.

Earlier mention was made of a ship sinking in a storm in Lake Michigan off the harbor at Sturgeon Bay, Wisconsin. In November of 1928 the S.S. Vestris, an ocean liner, 300 miles out of New York harbor, sank off the Virginia Capes. Passengers were lost and a consignment of three White Eagle toursters being sent to the Argentina Auto Show in Buenos Aires, went down with the ship. Each tourster was in a single large wood box, the entirety weighing three and one-half to four tons. In a court hearing after the sinking it was determined that, whereas, this shipment had nothing to do with the liner sinking, when it did tilt and sink these heavy crates shifted adding to the rapidity of the calamity.

The top of the line, White Eagle seven passenger sedan, in the Model 126 had an elongated wheelbase of 139 inches. This luxurious car had much standard equipment including silk window curtains, and silk plush or broadcloth upholstery. Kissel advertised that it had a top speed of 100 miles an hour.

The Seven Passenger Sedan

This White Eagle, Model 8-126 Speedster, had the large straight eight engine. It was the ultimate in the development of the line of Speedsters.

This factory picture of the All Year Coupe Roadster illustrated its folding top, as earlier introduced, in its 8-95 model, which was a successor to its 8-80, at least in its similar engine displacement of 247 cubic inches. Kissel also offered a solid top Coupe Roadster of quite similar appearance. All body styles of the Model 8-95 could also be gotten in a six-cylinder version, the model 6-73.

Chapter Eight

Kissel in the
Economic Collapse

The production figures for 1929 showed a further decrease to a total of 899 vehicles, compared to 1,069 in 1928. Of these, the passenger cars totaled 701, down from 848 in the prior year. Trucks and commercial cars totaled 198, down very slightly from the 221 of the 1928 model year. Thus, it can be seen that about one in every four vehicles was now of the commercial type. Included in the passenger car listing were 275 taxicabs, both the standard six as model 67-B, and the smaller 6-73 called model 57-B in the taxicab. It was also called their Junior Taxicab.

G.A. Kissel gave his figures for the total automobile production in the United States for 1928. This figure came to 4,630,000 cars and trucks. These vehicles in 1928 averaged a cost of $876 retail. Thus, Kissel, with its low end retail cost of $1,600 and a high of $4,000 was in the considerably higher cost range.

Also, in 1928 there were 24,750,000 motor cars and trucks registered in the United States, and the latter owned 78 percent of all the motor vehicles in the world.

The 1929 models were again shown at the New York National Auto Show. The Kissel brothers were in attendance showing their models and making contacts with their dealers. There were representatives of their sixes, the 6-73, the eights in the newly designated standard 8-95, and the new for the 1929 year, the 8-126.

But what they really wanted to show were their new Bradfield taxicabs with many body styles including a Victoria with the driver in an open front compartment, and in six and eight-cylinder engine sizes. As with all Kissel cars, these had a touch of beauty with an elegant finish, and in the appropriate taxicab colors of yellow and black. Hopes for a successful 1929 sales year unquestionably hinged on the potential sales of the Bradfield taxicabs, and the ongoing sales of their National Kissel motor cars for funeral directors.

Always hopeful, at least in his public expressions, was G.A. Kissel, fresh from his invigorating visit at the auto show in New York, with his statement, "Never before in the history of the world's largest, yet infant industry, was there more reason to look favorably upon the future than there is at the present time, that is the consensus of opinion of the manufacturers." Mr. Kissel also felt that there were two important deductions and trends to be made from the show. The first was that the American car was the most desirable in the world. The other point was that the prevailing tendencies were for larger and

Elegance and generous size were apparent in the 1929 National Kissel Hearse Ambulance in its top of the line Model 90-B, with an extended wheelbase of 162 inches, and the straight eight 126 engine. It featured a wide 40-inch rear loading door, with low positioned loading platform for easy access with heavy caskets. The casket table, flower tray, instrument panel, window and door mouldings were of select walnut. High quality silver finished hardware gave it an added touch of richness. Upholstery in genuine leather or silk mohair was offered.

The sturdy Kissel chassis is seen in the extended frame of the 1929 National Kissel Hearse model. It featured one-piece frame construction and heavy tubular cross members. The inset picture showed how the springs were mounted in rubber as was the engine, and other points of the chassis.

more comfortable automobiles. One cannot escape the hope and conviction that Mr. Kissel felt that his large and luxurious Kissels would fill this need. Mr. Kissel enjoyed the company of Ralph De Palma, the famous race driver, in looking over the exhibits in New York. De Palma further showed his regard for the Kissel automobile by purchasing one for his personal car, and then motoring with it to Hartford, Wisconsin, to be hosted by the Kissel brothers, Will and George, and to look over the factory.

Bradfield Motors announced in February of 1929 that they had been authorized to increase their capitalization stock from $250,000 to one million dollars. This information ran in all the Chicago papers at the time. While authorization for this increase was granted, it is not at all clear what amount of shares really were sold, and certainly not fulfilling these high expectations. It was further hoped that by having the experienced and respectable Mr. H. Bradfield, Elmer Knox, and George Daubner, all experienced taxicab people in engineering, management and sales, that success might be anticipated.

Bearing out these hopes was the large order for 500 new town car style taxicabs placed by an organization in New York. This was the Five Borough Fleet Owners Organization for these 500 vehicles and valued at a 1.25 million dollars. This organization was reported to control nearly one-half of all the taxicabs in operation in New York City at the time. The story survives that Kissel came out on the short end of the deal with this New York order. Kissel produced 275 taxicabs in 1929, invested their overhead in getting them produced in the Hartford factory, and then there were difficulties in getting paid by the depression-stressed taxicab fleet owners.

In 1929, Hartford was a small attractive city of 4,500 population. It remains so today with population still under 10,000. Visiting groups came to the Kissel factory, such as funeral directors from the Chicago area, to see the manufacture of their ambulance hearses. New in Hartford then was the Schwartz ballroom, advertised as the largest and most beautiful ballroom in the state of Wisconsin. Architecturally the building is of a unique octagonal design, with a huge ballroom floor.

Kissel would cater parties there for its visiting clients. The original Schwartz ballroom, with succeeding ownerships, exists today much the same as it did in 1929, but with one major exception. The newly laid floor, in 1928, was covered with a new synthetic material. This surface did not hold up. It contained a glue material which softened with use and stuck to the shoes of the dancing couples. This floor was removed and it was replaced with a fine hardwood surface.

Kissel was a beautiful car. An earlier account of a Berlin "beauty" show was given. There was one also in the summer of 1929 in Madrid, Spain, where a Kissel model 8-126 White Eagle beat out the likes of Citroen, Fiat, Cadillac, Oakland, Paige, and Studebaker. By standards of beauty and general appearance, Kissel was ahead of its time.

The year 1929 was a watershed in the history of the automobile. In spite of the dramatic downturn in automobile production that was to follow, this year saw a huge automobile production of 5,337,087, which was a million more than in the previous year and a record that was not to be surpassed for another 20 years. Output had dropped to 1,331,860 by 1932 at the depth of the depression. In 1929 the ratio of closed cars to open was 9:1, the opposite of the 1919 figure. In spite of the large drop in the manufacture of automobiles between 1929 and 1932 motor vehicle registrations dropped only 10 percent, meaning there were more older cars in use.

But there were ominous signs of the economic collapse highlighted by the stock market crash of November 1929. It hit the small manufactures, like Kissel, the hardest.

Wall Street, on September 13, 1929, suspecting the impending collapse, was countering this with reassurances that "hysterical rantings against speculations are absurd. The major stock exchanges and investment bankers have waged an unremitting war against improprieties. They subject all securities to the most rigid inspections before listing them for sale, and they keep constant check on the soundness of an issue."

By December 13, 1929 a Wall Street writer was saying that, "The conditions of the present and the panics of 1907 and 1921 rest on a false analogy. Furthermore, the New York

Stock Exchange, working in the interest of the investing public, has recently demanded from its members complete daily reports on stocks borrowed, from whom and for whose account, all stocks loaned, and a list of stocks they failed to deliver. Apparently, every effort is being made to protect legitimate investors and discourage professional manipulation."

What several other sizable businesses in Hartford did in 1929, and which Kissel did not, at least that early, was to merge or manage to be purchased by other larger competing businesses.

In October 1929 the Hartford Canning Company was bought out by Libby, NcNeil, and Libby of Chicago. Several owners later this plant was taken over by the Hartford Heritage Auto Museum, home now for the Kissel marque, and the subject of this story.

The Westphal Condensary, the large milk processing plant in Hartford, sold out to the much larger Luick Dairy Company of Milwaukee, which in turn later became an acquisition of the Kraft Cheese Company of Chicago.

One automobile related industry that expressed enthusiasm rather than dismay over the dwindling auto market was the B.F. Goodrich Rubber Company of Akron, Ohio. Their spokesman was confident that, based on past experience, their replacement tire business increased with decreased new auto sales, and there apparently were greater profits to be realized in the replacement tire market than the new tires furnished to auto manufacturers.

There was virtually no print advertising for Kissel in the latter half of 1929, reflecting their lessening fortunes and especially their financial problems. This was in contrast to the large, often full-page ads appearing for models of the large manufacturers such as Ford and Chevrolet.

The first public description of the 1930 Kissel model cars came in connection with the January, 1930 auto show held in New York City. Here, Kissel again exhibited its new models. There were four models in the 6-73 line, eight in the 8-95 line, and eight in the 8-126 line. Prices ranged from $1,595 to $3,895. This was certainly a wide spread of prices, covering the scale from high moderate to moderately expensive automobiles.

The changes in the 1930 Kissel lines were mostly cosmetic. For instance, the Deluxe Brougham Sedan was higher, longer, and four inches wider. The interiors were sumptuous, including a glove compartment. It was then not called glove compartment. Rather, it was described as a little compartment with a hinged door on the dash creating a space for gloves, tools, cigarettes, etc.

This was to be the last appearance of a Kissel at the New York Show. G.A. Kissel in this year was not making optimistic predictions for Kissel. Rather, he reviewed the past Kissel innovative features, some patented and some not. For the most part, Kissel patents covered engineered metal machined parts and not the constant body styling changes that Kissel was making. Exceptions would have been the body concept changes in producing the convertible tops for passenger cabs and the truck cabs.

The auto industry was extolling the benefits of all steel bodies for passenger safety, body quietness, and such. Kissel was continuing with its wooden frames. They were renowned for their body configurations and finishes over steel or aluminum. These were trip hammered and hand fit and molded over their custom fit body frames made out of hardwoods, oak and ash, among others. But Kissel was wedded to its past, not able to compete anymore in sales with its passenger cars, but hoping to do better where hand craftsmanship might be better displayed and appreciated such as in their elaborately fitted out hearses, adaptable to ambulance use through some additions and conversions, and their Bradfield taxicabs.

If misery liked company, Kissel had this in abundance. Most of the small independent auto manufacturers did not survive this period of economic depression. Figures released by the United States Department of Commerce taken from the 1930 United States census are revealing. At this time there remained only 162 auto manufacturing plants and this included plants making specialty trucks. This number, in turn, was to dwindle considerably in the succeeding few years.

The first public announcement of what was going on behind the scenes at the Kissel Motor Car Company regarding its front wheel drive plans and those of the Ruxton, appeared in June 1930. This was just after the 1930 Indianapolis 500 Memorial Day race in which the winner had driven a front wheel drive racer at 100.448 miles an hour. In reporting this event, Kissel made mention of the fact that they were involved in the production of a front wheel drive automobile.

For the 1930 model year Kissel manufactured 63 of their model 6-73, 236 of their model 95, 92 of their model 8-126, and 285 of their model 67 taxicabs. But they only sold 221 total vehicles. Of these, 93 were passenger cars, 77 funeral cars, just 49 taxicabs, and 2 trucks.

As late as August 29, 1930, Kissel was announcing closure of its plant for a week, with the stated intention of making changes in the plant to take care of a much larger daily production of cars. They stated all of these would be front wheel drive.

The next public announcement by Kissel came on September 19, 1930 when the Kissel Motor Car Company admitted that a friendly receivership of the company was underway.

G.A. Kissel explained that this action was taken, "To work out a 'most unpleasant situation,' left through failure of certain eastern interests to meet pledges and signed obligations. It is a friendly receivership and the company is working in conjunction with Mr. Melvin A. Traylor of Chicago, trustee of the Kissel bonds, who is cooperating with the A.C. Allyn Company of Chicago, which originally marketed the securities."

Mr. G.A. Kissel continued, "Such action was necessary because of the falling through of a deal between our company and Archie M. Andrews and the New Era Company of New York." This deal stipulated that the Kissel Company was to build a minimum of 1,500 front wheel drive cars under Ruxton patents, owned and controlled by New Era Motors.

"It further stated that the Kissel Company would have to build transmissions and parts for the Ruxton front wheel drive, in addition to the cars the company was already manufacturing. This included funeral cars, taxicabs, and Kissel passenger cars."

According to G.A. Kissel, Mr. Andrews advanced $100,000 and allowed the Kissel Company to go ahead with and prepare for the new program, but later refused to pay the balance, namely $150,000 which the arrangement called for. The reason given by Mr. Andrews for not concluding the payments called for, it was said, was that he was unable to raise the funds because of stock market conditions.

"The trust mortgage," [sic] added Mr. Kissel, "amounted originally to $750,000, of which almost $250,000 in principal has already been paid. The only default under the mortgage was the company's failure to pay about $18,000 in interest which became due in the past April."

The 1929/1930 White Eagle Phaetons were favorite personal cars in the Kissel family.

So, the same financial problems of Mr. Archie Andrews that so adversely affected the Kissel Motor Car Company also existed right inside the Kissel Company itself, namely their inability to meet their last interest payment, with a very substantial mortgage remaining, and at a time that their sales had plummeted badly.

Mr. Kissel announced further, that, "Under the reorganization plan it is further intended to diversify manufacturing in the Kissel plants, building several different lines, and contracting with several companies to handle sales and finances. The manufacture of Kissel passenger cars will be continued, but they will be built on the front wheel drive principle, and on a strictly custom built basis."

Mr. Kissel, while not mentioning it by name, was referring to the Moon Motor Car Company in St. Louis, Missouri, as one of the large companies he was contracting with for the manufacture of these front wheel drives.

But, two months later in November 1930, the Moon Company was also declaring bankruptcy. Application for a federal receiver for the Moon Motor Car Company was denied by a federal judge who saw, "No reason to

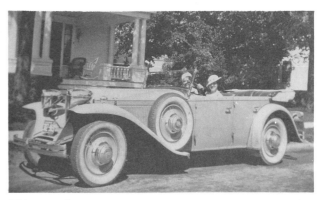

This scene from 1930, displayed the Ruxton, in a Phaeton model with the top down. Members of the Kissel family owned several Ruxtons. The marked resemblance to the White Eagle Phaeton of the same period might add credence to the claim that Kissel manufactured a few Phaeton bodies for the Ruxton effort. One obvious difference is the presence of the "Cat Eye" head lamps on the Ruxton.

appoint a federal receiver to sell 35 to 40 Ruxton cars." This may have been exaggerated on the downward side, but so, likely, also were reports that the Moon Company manufactured about 200 to 300 or more Ruxton cars.

If ever there was confusion it exists today in the true facts of the Kissel involvement in the production of the Ruxton front drive automobile. This was a very financially stressful time

This Ruxton was exhibited as a Roadster, with a rumble seat, and distinctive "Cat Eye" headlamps. Picture courtesy of Automobile Quarterly 1969.

at the Kissel Motor Car Company. Much of what could have been helpful here in the way of records was thrown out by a succession of owners of the old Kissel plant, most of which were connected with the outboard motor industry. Herman Palmer gave the number of Ruxtons assembled at Kissel as 26. He gave this figure several decades later on a taped recording. Of these George Kissel kept a Roadster and Will Kissel one of the two Phaetons which were built by changing Roadster panels shipped from Baker Raulang Company of Cleveland, Ohio, custom body builder, to accommodate rear doors. An outsize wheel cutout was required for each side panel. The Will Kissel Phaeton survives today after a succession of owners, starting with the early collector, D. Cameron Peck, who also bought the George Kissel Roadster.

The original contract with the New Era Motors Company, headed by Archie Andrews called for Kissel to build transmissions for the Ruxton. This was a very hectic and trying time in the Kissel organization. There is no evidence that they made any transmissions.

To compound the confusion, in the early 1950s when Will Kissel made his scrapbook entries he wrote that Kissel did not make any bodies for the Ruxton effort. With the above detailed information and the ability of the Kissel body shop to improvise, it stands true then that Kissel made some Ruxton bodies and that the recollection by Will Kissel was incorrect. William Muller, the designer of the front wheel drive Ruxton, might be relied on for useful information. He reported the number of Ruxtons built as 350, all assembled at the Moon Motors Company in St. Louis, Missouri, and excepting the 26 referred to earlier as having been assembled at the Kissel Motor Company.

As mentioned, it was late in 1930 that Kissel made public its dealings with Archie Andrews and its part in the production of the Ruxton automobile. This story has been much written about elsewhere, but some of the story will be recounted here because of its intertwining in the affairs of the Kissel Motor Car Company.

Archie Andrews, of English origin, was an entrepreneur involved in the financial world. In 1929 he formed the New Era Motors, Inc.

The short lived Ruxton of 1930 and 1931 was shown in a sedan model, illustrating its low profile compared to a contemporary model.

with the purpose of manufacturing the Ruxton automobile. The problem was he did not possess a factory and he intended to produce the Ruxton in existing automobile manufacturing plants.

The car was named after a man by the name of Ruxton, who was on his board of directors, and presumably possessed with some wealth. The implied wish was that by naming the new vehicle after Mr. Ruxton, the latter would be generous in supporting this venture. This, however, did not take place.

As mentioned, the front wheel design for the Ruxton was the work of William Muller. Muller worked for the Edward G. Budd Manufacturing Company of Philadelphia which made automobile bodies. While there, Muller built a prototype of a front wheel drive car, body by Budd, and with a six-cylinder engine by Studebaker. This happened in 1928. The first Ruxton, a sedan, developed after the formation of New Era Motors had the Studebaker engine replaced with a Continental motor. The body, again, was by the Budd Company, with subsequent roadster bodies by Baker-Raulang.

Since the New Era Motors did not have its own production plant, in his attempt to secure a manufacturer Andrews made overtures aimed at the Hupp Motor Car Company, Gardner, Marmon, Jordan and Stutz. His search ended with the Moon Company of St. Louis, Missouri, and the Kissel Motor Car Company of Hartford, Wisconsin. The Muller designed front wheel drive had the unique split transmission which better spread the weight and permitted a shorter hood than had the contemporary front wheel drive in the Cord, which beat the Ruxton to the market in 1929 with the first units. During a brief early association with the Moon Company, Andrews and Muller took over control of this company as officers.

It was a similar concern on the part of G.A. Kissel and his Kissel Motor Car Company that Archie Andrews would take control of their business that eventually caused them to arrange their receivership. Kissel was desperate for funds to continue to operate, and was fearful that Andrews would show cause that they were not fulfilling their part of the contract by their failure to produce Ruxtons in sufficient numbers.

A recent roster in the Classic Car Club of America showed six members owning a Ruxton automobile. Mr. Delyle Beyer, active in the C.C.C.A., was a former Ruxton owner. He recalls that for a time he owned the so called Alligator, having purchased it from Mr. Cameron Peck. Before that, it was an early prototypal model belonging to the engineer behind this front wheel project, Mr. William Muller. It had a Dodge Roadster body, altered to fit the second prototypal Ruxton chassis built.

Thus, with the termination of the affairs with the New Era Motors Company and the Ruxton automobile and the subsequent Kissel bankruptcy in September of 1930, we have come to the end of the Kissel story, at least as it regards the Kissel Motor Car Company.

Chapter Nine

The "Gold Bug"
and Its Successors

A special section of the Kissel story is being devoted to a review of the Kissel Speedster, and a succession of vehicles of the roadster or coupe roadster types. Emerging in 1917, the Kissel Speedster and these other vehicles will briefly be followed through the closing of the Kissel Motor Car Company in 1930.

The concept of this kind of roadster with a "racer cut" for its sides and a bumble bee or turtle back rear deck was developed from a prototype designed in 1917 through the combined efforts of Fred Werner at the Kissel Motor Car Company, and Conover Silver in New York City. William L. Kissel, always interested in styling, was also at hand to help with this project. Silver, the Kissel dealer in New York, and who also handled the Apperson, was much interested in imprinting his ideas of style and appearance into these automobiles. He was influenced by the specialty auto coach makers in his area, and also by some of the elite imported vehicles which could be seen on the streets of New York.

As mentioned earlier, by January of 1918, the Kissel Silver Special line, together with their Tourster, and their seven-passenger Touring car were being shown at the New York Auto Dealers Association Show held in the Grand Central Palace. Factory literature from the period shows the Speedster as a four-passenger vehicle, by virtue of the extra seating provided by the outrigger seats that could be pulled out from the sides of the rear deck compartment. These so-called "suicide seats," which Silver had conceived for Kissel and Apperson were questionably safe, impractical, and did not long remain as an option.

The early Speedster engine had the slightly smaller three and one-half by five inch motor that had existed before in their 6-38 models. This was shortly enlarged to the 61 brake horsepower motor with the three and five-sixteenths inch bore and five and one-half inch stroke. It had a 124-inch wheelbase and wire wheels by Houk. It remained in existence until 1924. This Speedster line created a sensation wherever it was shown. The public was fascinated with it, and its buyers included many sports and entertainment figures.

The Speedster continued with minor variations. By 1920 Kissel had dropped the Silver portion of the name. In 1921 it was shown in a factory picture as a two/four passenger vehicle with spare wheels on the sides, two step plates, and an affixed optional rear trunk. There were graceful bicycle-type fenders which Kissel called "sport" fenders. The Pantasote top had round side windows, and a rear oval window 13 inches across.

Again a factory picture from 1922 shows no major changes. The headlamps are bullet shaped, and were to become drum-shaped the next year. There was a single step plate, double indented, replacing the full running boards used before 1921. These Speedsters weighed 2,700 pounds and they were reported to achieve 13 to 16 miles to a gallon of fuel. The top price was now $3,750 reflecting the immediate World War inflationary period, and which was to rapidly decline thereafter.

The year 1924 was notable for Kissel in that they introduced their Enclosed Speedster. The auto market was changing from a preponderance of open cars to enclosed vehicles. Kissel met this need with the introduction of this model. Then in 1925, Kissel brought out its first eight-cylinder engine, a straight eight. It was the 3-H engine, and was one of many made by this company for the auto industry at the time. Kissel considerably reworked this engine to their own exacting specifications with their own Lynite pistons, connecting rods, and aluminum head and crankcase. So if Kissel gave scant or no public recognition to the Lycoming Company they were perhaps quite justified in claiming this engine to be their own, and because the final product was truly a Kissel. The Speedsters were then offered in the sixes and in the new eights, called 8-75.

Kissel had pioneered as early as 1914 with the concept of an all weather, All Year car with its Detachable Top. Then, in 1926, they produced their All Year Coupe Roadsters. These featured, in addition to a front seating compartment, a rear deck rumble seat for two. With the top up, it was cradled and supported by an additional member, an inverted U-shaped bar, positioned at the rear of the front seat compartment. The same feature of a rumble seat was now also appearing in the four-passenger speedsters.

In 1928 Kissel had gone to using the Kissel 8-90 White Eagle Deluxe description for some specially fitted out deluxe models with engine bore slightly increased. Kissel now also made a smaller eight, the 8-80, and the Speedsters were available in these also.

New for 1929 was the top of the line 8-126 with 115 horsepower and advertised to be capable of 100 miles an hour. With this engine the Kissel Speedster saw its ultimate development. In this year the 6-55 model was dropped. Retained was the small six, earlier the 6-70, and now named model 6-73. The Speedster was also available in the model 8-95, which had earlier been the 8-90.

There were no changes in 1930 when passenger car production had all but ceased with the greater emphasis being placed on the manufacture of the Bradfield taxis and the National Kissel Hearse Ambulances.

There are no exact figures available on the number of Kissel Speedsters ever built. However, the number was not large. Will Kissel, in his memoirs written around 1952, estimated that the Kissel Motor Car Company manufactured just about 50 Speedsters for the model year 1918. He gave as his reason for the slim number the effort that was needed for the production of trucks for the military. There are no specific figures available for the other years. Rather they were incorporated in the figures given for the different engine sizes.

The Gold Bug and Kissel Speedsters in other colors caught the fancy of the public that was looking for something new and bold after the First World War. In addition to those well known figures already mentioned, it numbered among its customers: Ruby Keeler, Mary Pickford, Douglas Fairbanks, Sr., Gladys George, Bebe Daniels, and Mabel Normand.

104

Chapter Ten

Kissel Motor Car Company
To Kissel Industries

As will become apparent, the Kissel Motor Car Company did not go directly into the Kissel Industries. There was a two-year hiatus, with little production of a product, and mostly legalities, before the Kissel Industries was established in September 1932. In between, from December 1931 to September 1932, the Kissel enterprise was in the hands of the bond holders committee which had the unenvious task of trying to satisfy the Kissel creditors. During this period of approximately nine months the Kissel concern was called the Kissel Company, as it no longer was the Kissel Motor Car Company.

A very small number of automobiles left over from the 1930 year production were sold as 1931 models. There was a demand for and continuing production of taxicabs that went into the Milwaukee market. In February of 1932 a fleet of 25 black and yellow painted Kissel taxicabs were driven as a unit to Milwaukee, where they were to be used by the Yellow Cab Company there. These taxicabs were built by Kissel in Hartford under the direction of the Taxi Manufacturing Corporation of America which owned the Yellow Cab Company in Milwaukee at that time. So these vehicles were produced by a small crew of workers in the Kissel plant after the legal closing of the Kissel plant and during the period of receivership activity. Mention was also made then, in February of 1932, of further preparations and plans for a new batch of taxicabs to be delivered to Milwaukee.

The question is often asked: Just how many Kissel cars were built during the 25 years of operation as the Kissel Motor Car Company? At times, much larger figures have been presented. But, the figure of 35,000, or slightly less would come closer to actuality. This would include all the passenger cars, trucks from 1909 on, funeral cars and taxicabs during the last few years of their existence.

The production numbers from 1920 to 1930 and the official closing of the Kissel plant are available from company records and should be fairly accurate. This number is 14,204, and add about 50 vehicles held over and sold at the end of 1930 into 1931. Those from 1916 through 1919 can be fairly well approximated based on available and accurate dollar sales records during these years. The approximation for this four-year segment then is 7,860 based on an average value of a Kissel at that time. The numbers from 1906 and model year 1907 through 1915 are more nebulous. Based on the first year production of 100 cars going to Jos. McDuffee in Chicago, and a high of 5,000 vehicles produced in 1915 with the enthusiasm over its Convertible Top All-Year Cars, and in between figures averaging about 1,500 cars per year, we come to the approximated figure for these years of 13,500. Bear in mind, Kissel never strove for high production numbers. Rather its emphasis was on quality of product, and a manufactured "custom built" product rather than just one that was assembled.

A long fleet of 1930 Bradfield taxicabs were lined up in the Kissel railroad yards awaiting shipment. Vehicles shown here had a soft front roof that could be folded back for the driver. Kissel also made taxicabs with totally enclosed roofs.

Will Kissel, in his scrapbook memoirs put down in 1952, gave some estimates of production figures. Whereas, his memory may have been dimmed somewhat by the passage of time, they generally agree with the above. This scrapbook, an invaluable record of a march through time of the Kissel Motor Car Company from its inception to 1930, was donated by his son, Robert Kissel, Sr., and his grandson, Robert, Jr., to the Hartford Heritage Auto Museum.

Accurate production figures were certainly kept in the business files of the Kissel Motor Car Company. Unfortunately, many of these just did not survive the ownership changes that took place in the Kissel plant as it went from the Kissel Industries of the 1930s to the purchase of the plant by the then West Bend Aluminum Company for the manufacture of outboard motor engines in 1944. With the subsequent ownership changes involving the purchase by the Chrysler Corporation and their Marine Division in 1965, and further, the purchase of the plant in 1984 by Bayliner Boats and their U.S. Marine Division, this activity necessitated the need for large manufacturing space and the discarding of the remnants of the previous Kissel Motor Car Company records and many old Kissel vehicle parts. Thus, a huge amount of Kissel engine and body parts were thrown out that would have been of considerable value to present day Kissel car collectors for their restoration efforts.

In January of 1958 the West Bend Company, successor to the West Bend Aluminum Company in name, turned over some of the Kissel records to the State of Wisconsin Historical Society. This has remained an important source of information on the Kissel, especially in regard to its dealership contracts, and Kissel patents. Outside of materials in private hands, the bulk of Kissel related materials is stored at the Hartford Heritage Auto Museum in Hartford, Wisconsin, present home of the Kissel, and about 15 Kissel cars, trucks, and fire trucks. The Kissel Kar Klub, operated out of this museum, is in contact with about 150 Kissel owners and friends of the Kissel. Understandably, with manufacture that ceased 60 years ago, there is a problem for the Kissel restorers in finding suitable parts for their restorations. In many cases, the Kissel owner must resort to the expensive alternative of having these parts custom built for his vehicle.

After the collapse of the Kissel Motor Car Company, there was a need to supply parts for the existing Kissel automobiles in the hands of present owners. In mid-1931 the service department was taken over by the Fuller-Johnson Company of Madison, Wisconsin.

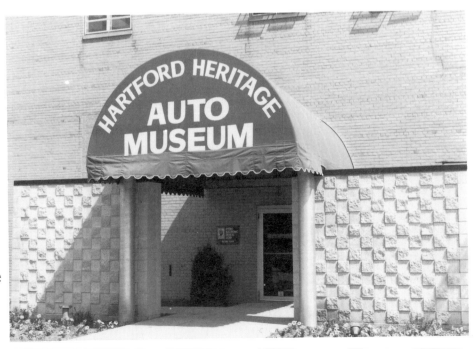

The Hartford Heritage Auto Museum is located at 147 N. Rural Street, in Hartford, Wisconsin. It has been in existence since 1986. It houses numerous models of Kissel automobiles, together with other domestic and imported vehicles.

Records show them to have originated in 1840, and were in 1930 manufacturers of gasoline and kerosene engines, and electric light plants. The same records show that in July 1930 they were also in the hands of their bond holders. What form of the company survived to take on this Kissel service work is not known. But it is then also not surprising to learn that in May of 1932 there was an announcement in Automobile Topics, that these interests were sold to W.C. Stewart of Freeport, Illinois. This organization was then designated to give service to all Kissel owners at the Kissel plant. However, it was stated, much of the parts store would be located in Freeport, Illinois. The logistical problem this must have caused is apparent. Somewhat later there was a small service in Kissel parts handled by Dallas Winslow who took over the leftover parts from the Stewart Company. He operated out of Connersville, Indiana. Still later, these found their way into the hands of a parts dealer in Oklahoma, and where the service ended.

The "unpleasant situation" which G.A. Kissel referred to was compounded by other entities trying to collect money from the now defunct Kissel Motor Car Company. On June 8, 1931 the Washington County Sheriff, and the district attorney of the same county, visited Hartford and Kissel for the purpose of levying against personal property of the Kissel Motor Car Company, for the collection of personal property tax amounting to $13,000. This drew reaction from a Milwaukee court judge who issued a restraining order against them from collecting such a tax without a written order of the court.

Then, in December of 1931 under proper court proceedings, as G. A. Kissel described it, the bond holders committee took over the properties, but were unable to arrange for the necessary cash requirements. The receivers were G.A. Kissel and Charles Davison of Fond du Lac, Wisconsin.

Thereafter, the Kissel interests continued under the name of the Kissel Company during this further period of limbo, at least as a descriptive legal entity was concerned. Then, in September of 1932, what had been the property of the Kissel Motor Car Company, followed by a bond holders tenure with some taxicab production by the Kissel Company, was bid on and taken over by the newly formed Kissel Industries. The officers for the Kissel Industries consisted of George A. Kissel, William L. Kissel, of the former Kissel Motor Car Company, and Blanche M. Kissel, wife of G.A. Kissel. As is apparent, the affairs of this new industry were back in the hands of the original founders of the Kissel Motor Car Company and a spouse.

Chapter Eleven

Kissel Industries

The Kissel Industries was incorporated in an attempt to continue the Kissel enterprise in their large factory, in some product that would get Kissel functioning again. The estate of Mr. Herman Palmer, the head mechanical engineer at Kissel for many years, has furnished the Hartford Heritage Auto Museum with blueprints and descriptions from this engineer for a railroad train that was to be manufactured at the Kissel plant. This train was designed to be manufactured to carry the United States mail. This train turned out to be the streamlined aluminum Burlington Zephyr, the first of its type. The date on this blueprint drawing is January 9, 1933, and it is highly detailed, consistent with the careful work of Herman Palmer. Included with these papers are specifications with detailed drawings covering 38 pages. This plan never got beyond his drawing board. Apparent factors were a lack of sufficient financing, plus the fact that Kissel lacked the necessary machinery and space, especially ceiling height, which would have been required for a project of this size.

The next activity of the Kissel Industries occurred in the fall of 1934. This was their attempt to get back into the automobile manufacturing business. They were proposing to build a car called the "Royale." Their efforts to proceed hinged on the need to secure a $200,000 loan through the Reconstruction Finance Corporation in Chicago. This organization was set up to help business in this post depression era of our economy. Mr. G. A. Kissel, former president of the Kissel Motor Car Company, attempted to secure the assistance of the then senator from Wisconsin, Robert M. LaFollette, Jr., in securing this loan. In trying

to plead his case before representatives of the Reconstruction Finance Corporation, Mr. Kissel reviewed the earlier history of the Kissel Motor Car Company.

This included the information on the organizational structure in 1906 when the auto company was formed. The original stock was owned by Louis Kissel, father, and sons, A.P. Kissel, O.P. Kissel, W. L. Kissel, G.A. Kissel, and attorney Mr. H.K. Butterfield.

As the company showed earnings, these earnings were capitalized until the company had 10,000 shares of common stock at a par value of $100 each. The common stock was still held by the same parties and considera-

Herman Palmer with his cello, at age 77, was profiled in a newspaper account. Palmer, as a youth came to Hartford with his cello, and he and his family played instruments throughout his career with the Kissel Motor Car Company.

ble surplus was shown on the books in excess of the preferred and common stock.

Later, O.P. Kissel, W. L. Kissel, and G. A. Kissel purchased the common stock of Mr. Butterfield, and the stock then continued to be held by the Kissels until in 1922 when ten percent was held by F. W. Thomas.

There was also $250,000 in the preferred stock authorized, but only about $90,000 of this was issued and held largely by local people.

Later, the bond issue secured by first mortgage on the plant and property in the amount of $750,000 was completely underwritten by A.C. Allyn and Company of Chicago. There was about $529,000 in bonds outstanding. The bond holders committee represented the bond holders in all proceedings.

Mr. George A. Kissel, then, in his proposal to the Reconstruction Finance Corporation, detailed some of the areas of eminence of the Kissel motor car, and the fact that there were still some 12,000 owners of Kissel automobiles.

What Kissel proposed to build with the assistance of the loan was an eight-cylinder automobile. It was to be light in weight, economical, somewhat streamlined, and finely polished as were all Kissel vehicles. Kissel proposed to build the body, hood, and vehicle front. The chassis was to be manufactured by the "R" company, as they then rather secretly referred to it. For whatever reason for the early secrecy about the R company, it actually turned out to be Reo Company. The engine was to be the Lycoming straight-eight which was in use by Kissel since 1925.

It was hoped to place this car on the market for $1,500, a price that would seem to be unrealistic in consideration of the prices needed by Kissel in earlier years with their elegantly constructed bodies. It was hoped to secure buyers from the pool of the 12,000 Kissel automobile owners, and the 1,200 established Reo dealers.

Kissel attempted to bolster its argument for the $200,000 loan with the information that it had leased one floor of about 55,000 square feet with the Simplex Shoe Manufacturing Company, which netted an income of over $5,000 per year. George Kissel further stated he was hopeful of leasing additional space in the factory for added income. If these figures sound insignificant, they were in light of the amount of loan they were attempting to secure. George Kissel went on to detail contracts that Kissel had closed with an unnamed Chicago company for machining auto replacement parts. These were for Ford, Chevrolet, Plymouth, and others. There was further a contract with A.L. Powell Power Company, to build eight cylinder motors for them. All of these plans came to naught. The Reconstruction Finance Corporation, which was to handle the loan, exchanged probing letters with George Kissel, all demanding information delving into the financial health of the Kissel Industries. In the end, the loan was declined and the hopes for a new Kissel automobile vanished. Today, a 1:6 scale wooden model of the rather aerodynamically styled "Royale" venture is on display at the Hartford Heritage Auto Museum in Hartford, Wisconsin, taking its place among restored Kissel automobiles.

With this the story of the Kissel automobile manufacturing enterprise ended. Of all the

This is the Royale. This 1:6 scale wooden model of the car was made by employees of the Kissel Motor Car Company in 1929 or 1930. It represented what Kissel had in mind for its car of the future. The efforts to produce it in 1934 came to naught for a lack of sufficient funds.

Kissel cars produced, there remain about 150 in existence today. And, of these, not all are well restored. The Kissel marque lives on, mostly through the activities of the Kissel Kar Klub which will be described in the epilogue.

The failed Royale automobile venture was followed with another Kissel Industries venture in September of 1935. After a very brief period of vending machine manufacture, Kissel started manufacturing wooden chairs. These wooden chairs were turned out in their facilities that had earlier made their wooden automobile body frames. These chairs were made of hardwoods, mostly in maple, and handsomely upholstered. They had a contract to sell 2,500 of these chairs through a Chicago outlet. This effort lasted less than a year.

At about the same time, in September 1935, Kissel Industries was awarded a contract by Sears, Roebuck, and Company of Chicago to produce outboard motors for them. Production was underway by April of 1936. These were mostly one-cylinder engines, but there were manufactured a lesser number of two-cylinder size. This outboard engine was called the Water Witch. The motor was designed by Sears engineers, but it had a water pump of Kissel design. Engine testing on water was done on the adjacent Rubicon River pond, and nearby Pike Lake. During the cold winter months testing was done at Hot Springs, Arkansas. Some of the machinery for this production came from revised leftover auto manufacturing stock. Kissel Industries had as many as 120 men in this production. There were some lean periods. There was a shutdown in 1938 with a note from the company that production would start up again in the spring of 1939. Later, this business did prosper, and in 1941 the company put out 33,000 outboard motors.

While successful, outboard engine production ceased completely in April of 1942, when the plant was turned over to lucrative war production making steel casings for torpedoes for the U.S. Navy. Kissel also had contracts with the U.S. Army, and the nature of this was kept rather secret from the public.

George Kissel had a sudden fatal cardiovascular collapse at age 61 in 1942. Brother Will Kissel stayed on with the company to furnish the military until Kissel Industries was sold to the West Bend Aluminum Company in 1944. This company then finished the military contracts and in addition made Elgin brand outboard motors for the Sears Roebuck and Company. The West Bend Company continued in existence until 1965 when they sold out to the Chrysler Corporation for their marine division which made outboard motors under their name until 1984 when they were sold to the U.S. Marine Division of Bayliner Boat Manufacturing Company which continues in the business of outboard manufacture with their engine, called the Force.

Epilogue

This closing section of the Kissel story should rightfully tell about the Kissel Kar Klub. This club has kept alive the Kissel automotive tradition by carefully maintaining a record of the remaining Kissels in the hands of these collectors.

Kissel owners and friends of the Kissel, together with former dealers and employees would meet from time to time, informally, often in connection with attendance at auto shows across the country. Through this interest, as early as 1954, there emerged the idea of setting up a club devoted to the Kissel marque. This, in turn, led to the formation of the Kissel Kar Klub in 1957. The alliteration in the use of the capital 'K' existing in the name Kissel was apparent in the title of the club. The Kissel Kar Klub limited its membership to owners of Kissel Motor Car Company, family members, and others with Kissel connections, such as former dealers.

Purposes of the Kissel Kar Klub were to maintain the identify of the Kissel, to help members with their restorations, and to be a sort of clearing house for interest and problems in this regard. Much of the activity also concerned proper identification of the existing Kissels through extant lists of serial numbers, helping to establish years of production of these vehicles. Due to the variability of accuracy of these records, this effort at times has met with limited success. The following were charter members of this club: William (Will) L. Kissel, patron; Gene Husting, correspondent; Ralph Dunwoodie, parts and service advisor and history; Dick Braund, antique auto restorer including Kissel, and a manufacturer of replica Duesenberg automobiles; and Jackson Barnhart, a longtime Kissel collector and whimsy-enjoying individual.

At first it was the idea to have the headquarters for this new club at the old Kissel factory quarters in Hartford. It was then used as an outboard motor factory by the Marine Division of the West Bend Company. The idea floundered. The next suggestion was that it be at the home of Will Kissel in Hartford. By this time Will was spending winters in the southern climates and would then not be the answer. What eventually emerged was a plan to have it at the home of Ralph Dunwoodie who was working in Hartford at this time. Copies of club records were kept by both Dunwoodie in Hartford, Wisconsin, and Gene Husting in Boston.

After a few more years Dunwoodie left Hartford for employment with Harrah Museum Collection in Reno, Nevada, and who was shortly to become its manager. All the records and correspondence were then handled by Gene Husting of Boston, and later of Long Island, New York.

Will was pleased that plans were for an organization that was informal, low key, and without election of officers, and without the need for regular meetings. In effect, Will Kissel became the honorary patron of the club and agreed to be listed as "Patron."

For the next 25 years Gene Husting was the official source of the Kissel Kar Klub newsletters and all correspondence with Kissel car owners. Gene carefully kept duplicate copies of all his correspondence and they have been handed over to the library of the Hartford Heritage Auto Museum. Gene has also been generous in supplying much Kissel memorabilia that have been invaluable in the preparation of the Kissel Story. He published, among other Kissel writings, a comprehensive work on the Kissel marque, which appeared in the September-October 1961 issue of the *Antique Automobile Club of America* magazine. It was condensed for the June 1971 issue of the prestigious *Automobile Quarterly* hardcover magazine.

Ralph Dunwoodie lived for a period, 1956 to 1962, in Hartford before joining the Harrah Museum Collection at Reno, Nevada, where he handled their restorations. He has remained an authority on Kissel, especially the mechanics and history of the vehicle. Today, he collects, maintains, and distributes information and researches the history of antique cars and trucks professionally out of his home in Sun Valley, Nevada.

Dick Braund has an auto restoring and classic auto manufacturing business in the village of Elroy, Wisconsin. Here he has produced beautiful Duesenberg car replicas. He has restored a number of Kissel automobiles, the last of which recently left his shops.

Will Kissel was a young man, just 27 years old, when he and his brother, George, started up the company that bore the Kissel name. He lived throughout the entire cycle of this family owned industry. The company came to an end in 1930, not recovering from the financial crash that began in November, 1929. Will Kissel remained semi-active in the successor proprietorship for 14 years when it existed during an early interval period followed by the Kissel Industries which was given over to the manufacture of numerous products, but chiefly the Water Witch outboard engines.

Will had a rather joyous flair for living, and it often manifested itself in the Kissel manufacturing business as fresh styling ideas. He died at the advanced age of 93 years on September 4, 1972.

Through the years the Kissel Kar Klub sent out periodic newsletters to Kissel car owners, former officers, and dealers of the firm, and family and friends of the Kissel organization. After 1980 the newsletter was again called the *Kisselgraph,* named after the very first publications at the onset of our participating in the First World War in 1918. After August of 1981, the headquarters of the club became the Hartford Chamber of Commerce, with Dale Anderson as its director. Since 1986 and the opening of the Hartford Heritage Auto Museum, this location has become the home of the Kissel Kar Klub and the Kissel antique car collection, together with other domestic and foreign vehicles.

The story of the Kissel automobile, as far as its management was concerned, revolved mainly around the brothers, George and Will Kissel. The father, Louis, undoubtedly had a positive influence on these sons and on their early development of the Kissel Motor Car Company prior to his death by gunshot wound in 1908.

As mentioned earlier, at the formation of the auto company in 1906, brother Otto was its first vice president. Shortly, it became obvious that his interests, and those of Adolph, lay not primarily in the auto business, but rather in the real estate industry, both city and rural. Otto and Adolph were certainly available to give financial counsel to the two brothers actively engaged in the

Will Kissel in 1955, and at age 76 years, was some ten years retired from the Kissel Industries. His effervescent smile was apparent.

affairs of the Kissel Motor Car Company. Also, Otto was a president of the First National Bank of Hartford, Wisconsin.

Orville Kissel, a son of Adolph Kissel, worked in Chicago with the Kissel agency run there by Harry Branstetter. He had also worked in the Denver Kissel agency.

Will Kissel had sons, Robert and William, Jr. Robert worked at the Kissel plant summers during the time he was going to college, as did Adolph's son, Lester, a prominent New York attorney, now retired. William, Jr., worked a longer period of time at the Kissel plant helping both his father, Will, and Uncle George. He later did accounting for the firm and stayed on with the business after it became Kissel Industries.

George Kissel was a compulsively hard worker. Yet, he was reported by a niece as being fun loving. In his off-time from work, he was frequently seen at the movies. His children, George, Jr., and Jane, received the attention of the parents and a personal maid and chauffeur. The drive and work-related stress in the life of George Kissel may have been a factor in his relatively early death at the age of 61 in 1942. However, this is conjecture, and the cause was surmised to be of cardiovascular origin, as it came on rapidly without warning while he was at work. His family did have the genes contributing to longevity, with the evidence that one sister lived to be 100 years of age, and the long life of brother Will. The father, Louis, was reported to be in robust health when he was shot at age 69 years.

Blanche Kissel, wife of George and later owner and active head of the Kissel Industries, was a free-spirited woman. She did not object to testing accepted conventions. She had a Kissel automobile in the 1920s that was painted in shades of sand and pistachio. She then had her vehicle license plates painted in the same shades of colors. After several warnings by traffic police, she consented to revert back to standard Wisconsin license plate colors. Blanche Kissel contributed to the running of the Kissel Industries, and more so after the death of her husband in 1942 until the plant was taken over by the West Bend Company.

William L. Kissel, known as Will to some, and more frequently as Bill, could be described as being friendly, approachable, and with an informal nature. He appears not to really have envied the top position in the Kissel Motor Car Company with minor exceptions. He certainly helped to ensure the stability of the company by remaining in the one position of secretary and treasurer for the entire life of the business. That he was inventive and interested in style and function can be gathered by the fact of his patenting with Fred Werner the Convertible Auto Body, and was in practice called the Convertible Top or Transformable Top. This became a part of their All-Year Car, and the most publicly acclaimed invention of the Kissel Motor Car Company. He remained active and healthy into late life. He never remarried after the loss of his wife, Elizabeth, while she was still quite young. In the early days of the Ruxton, he could be seen driving his Ruxton Touring car, one of only two built. Later, he was to own an early model of the Ford Thunderbird. He would be seen on his way to the Hartford Country Club where he was an active member until late in his life. Absent from his Thunderbird were the golf bag fender racks which were a staple option for the famous Kissel Speedsters.

118

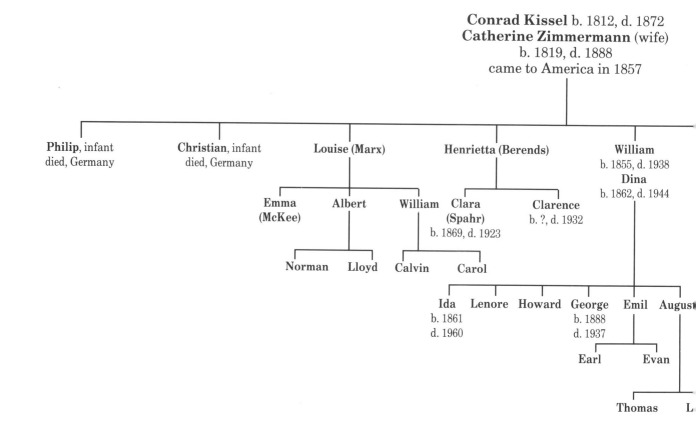

Conrad Kissel b. 1812, d. 1872
Catherine Zimmermann (wife)
b. 1819, d. 1888
came to America in 1857

Philip, infant
died, Germany

Christian, infant
died, Germany

Louise (Marx)

Henrietta (Berends)

William
b. 1855, d. 1938
Dina
b. 1862, d. 1944

Emma
(McKee)

Albert

William

Clara
(Spahr)
b. 1869, d. 1923

Clarence
b. ?, d. 1932

Norman   Lloyd

Calvin   Carol

Ida
b. 1861
d. 1960

Lenore   Howard

George
b. 1888
d. 1937

Emil   August

Earl   Evan

Thomas   L

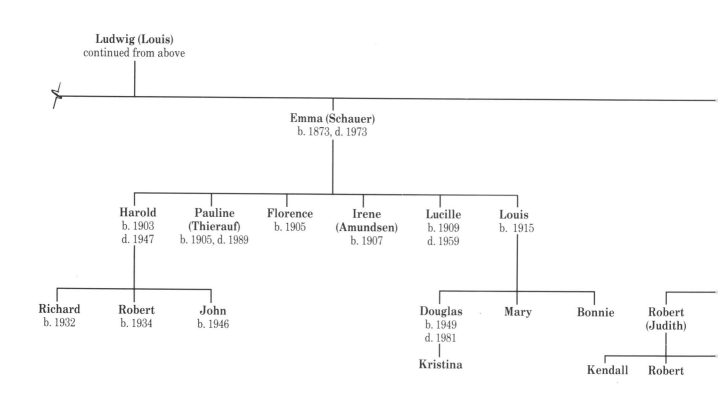

Ludwig (Louis)
continued from above

Emma (Schauer)
b. 1873, d. 1973

Harold
b. 1903
d. 1947

**Pauline
(Thierauf)**
b. 1905, d. 1989

Florence
b. 1905

**Irene
(Amundsen)**
b. 1907

Lucille
b. 1909
d. 1959

Louis
b. 1915

Richard
b. 1932

Robert
b. 1934

John
b. 1946

Douglas
b. 1949
d. 1981

Mary   Bonnie

**Robert
(Judith)**

Kristina

Kendall   Robert

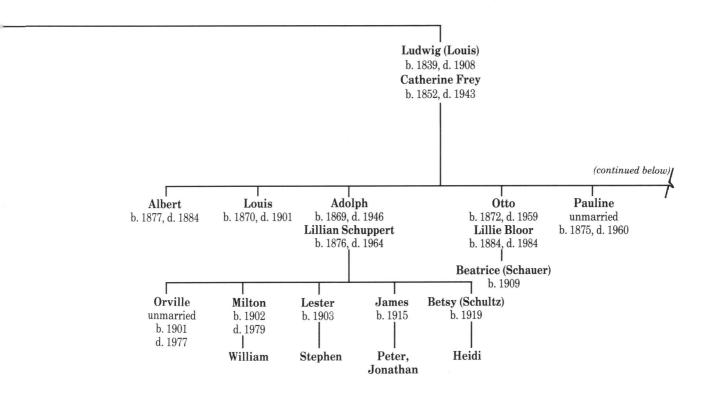

Ludwig (Louis)
b. 1839, d. 1908
Catherine Frey
b. 1852, d. 1943

(continued below)

Albert
b. 1877, d. 1884

Louis
b. 1870, d. 1901

Adolph
b. 1869, d. 1946
Lillian Schuppert
b. 1876, d. 1964

Otto
b. 1872, d. 1959
Lillie Bloor
b. 1884, d. 1984

Pauline
unmarried
b. 1875, d. 1960

Beatrice (Schauer)
b. 1909

Orville
unmarried
b. 1901
d. 1977

Milton
b. 1902
d. 1979

Lester
b. 1903

James
b. 1915

Betsy (Schultz)
b. 1919

William

Stephen

**Peter,
Jonathan**

Heidi

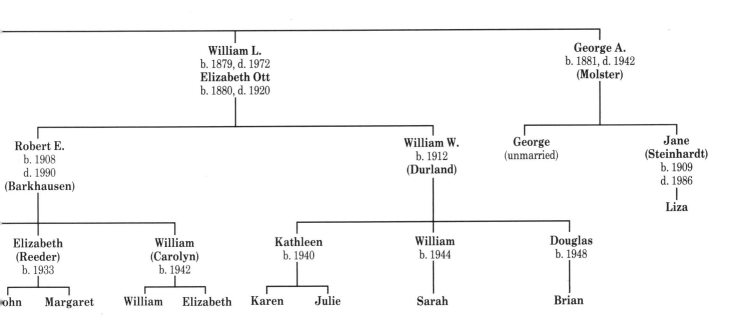

William L.
b. 1879, d. 1972
Elizabeth Ott
b. 1880, d. 1920

George A.
b. 1881, d. 1942
(Molster)

Robert E.
b. 1908
d. 1990
(Barkhausen)

William W.
b. 1912
(Durland)

George
(unmarried)

**Jane
(Steinhardt)**
b. 1909
d. 1986

Liza

**Elizabeth
(Reeder)**
b. 1933

**William
(Carolyn)**
b. 1942

Kathleen
b. 1940

William
b. 1944

Douglas
b. 1948

ohn   **Margaret**

William   Elizabeth

Karen   Julie

Sarah

Brian

Index